Shadow Girl

sightline books

The Iowa Series in Literary Nonfiction

Patricia Hampl & Carl H. Klaus, series editors

Deb Abramson
Shadow Girl

A Memoir of Attachment

University of Iowa Press ψ Iowa City

University of Iowa Press, Iowa City 52242
Printed in the United States of America
Design by Richard Hendel
http://www.uiowa.edu/uiowapress

"Secret Body" first appeared in *Under the Sun* 6
(Summer 2001); "Proof: A Preface" first appeared
in *River Teeth* 2 (Spring 2001).

The publication of this book was generously
supported by the University of Iowa Foundation.

Printed on acid-free paper

Cataloging-in-Publication data on file at the Library of Congress.

02   03   04   05   06   C   5   4   3   2   1

Contents

Acknowledgments

I could not have written this book without the cooperation of my family, who have respected my memory and perspective and kept themselves from asking too many questions.

Alexandra Harrison helped me to find the stories and see that they mattered. Lisa Knopp encouraged me when I had the beginnings of a book, and the MFA program at Goucher College provided much-needed guidance and support. My writer's group — Dale Gasque, Anne Holbrook, Laura McCaffrey, Susan Ritz, and Robin Sales — offered companionship and insights as it began to take shape. Steve Gross and Jerry Kisslinger read my work carefully and responded thoughtfully. Eliza Thomas gently pushed me to keep at it when I was ready to throw in the towel.

My agent, Kim Witherspoon, shared her editorial wisdom and helped this book find the right hands. I am grateful as well to her assistant, Alexis Hurley, for all her behind-the-scenes work.

I could not have dreamed up more attentive and respectful editors than Holly Carver, Carl Klaus, and Prasenjit Gupta.

Finally, for his unwavering support, thanks to Joel Sackman, who knew I was a writer long before I did and told me this day would come.

Proof: A Preface

We are story tellers, story seekers. We lean into the promise of narrative the way dogs lean into the wind, imagining a meal from a faint whiff of hide, detecting some kind of trouble in the distant rumble of an engine. It is our way of making sense of the world. We guess that the policeman who issued a ticket when a warning would have sufficed must have had an argument with his wife this morning; we assume that a household robbery makes a family more cautious about locking up; we believe that getting a prescription filled can create a whole new you, nothing the same from that point on. One thing occurs, then something else occurs after that as a result. *What happens next?* we are always asking. And *why?* A story develops, the weaving together of circumstance and explanation. There is the rhythm of cause and effect, cause and effect; they are links in a chain of understanding.

Yet when I think about the story of my life, try as I will to find one, this kind of narrative, shaped by a sturdy armature of singular events, eludes me. There are no watershed incidents that divide my existence neatly into before and after. The moments that now surface from my memory do not seem to have led me incontrovertibly in one direction or another, or to have drastically altered the texture of my world. Rather, they are exemplary tales, underscoring patterns that already existed, pointing to ways of thinking and being that were already lodged firmly in place. On their own, they are susceptible to taking on larger significance; but I know that they are in some way representative stories, isolated now from the seemingly infinite series of similar incidents — though I may not remember them — of which they were originally a part. They are emblematic rather than definitive, illustrative rather than generative. They are proof.

I am not arguing for nature above nurture, nor am I contending that my life is a landscape endlessly repeating itself like the background in a cheap cartoon, the same wobbly palm tree and cluster of brown rocks appearing over and over no matter how fast and furiously the character runs. Of course the terrain of my experience took on new shape and texture. Of course I grew and developed and turned into the person I am right now. Of course the context in which I came to know myself helped forge that understanding. But change did not occur in identifiable and irreversible surges, and it did not come in response to the specific cluster of details and effects that made up any one moment in time, or through astonishing bursts of enduring insight that never clouded over or slipped away. It occurred slowly, organically, with a steady inevitability, the way a boulder erodes under the relentless pressure of a river, the way a plant bends itself toward nurturing light.

This model, of course, has less drama than the traditional life story, but it is truer to my own experience of myself and the world around me. Narrative has always been difficult for me; it feels like an imposition, a contrived structure. The short stories I used to write were often filled with carefully wrought descriptions and illuminating details, but nothing ever happened in them. I am by nature more prone to reflection than action; I have always believed that the real work of being takes place deep inside. It somehow doesn't seem right that my psyche could be tamed or twisted by an event, a piece of dialogue, the sight of something profound.

So what replaces the spark and pace of narrative drive? How do I make meaning out of a life with no strong plot? Through a series of overlapping hunches that are bolstered by memory, impressions that in and of themselves are fixed but in each other's presence cause tension and ripple. Often they are contradictory. *You were a tomboy*, I tell myself. *You were a fearless child. And here is the proof: You ran with boys around the backyard, getting banged up and dirty; you dug up earthworms to feed the bird with the broken wing.* But then I can just as easily call up evidence to the contrary: *You couldn't stand it when your shirt came untucked, when the shoes in your closet were not lined up in a perfect row. At seven you were panicked about going to college; you asked your mother how you would ever find your way around campus. You were a shy and halting girl.*

And from this jumble of impressions, I begin to see that over time, some kind of story emerges. It is a quiet tale, a little messy, driven by a mysterious and invisible and sometimes wayward engine. Finding its architecture can be tricky work.

This process does not come naturally to me, and sometimes the inconsistencies and dead ends are frustrating. I am susceptible to the allure of easy answers; I want to be able to turn the past inside out and see for certain what gave my life its shape — as if personal history were some perfectly constructed garment, a bright thread binding all the pieces together in a clear and steady path, no fraying edges, no loosening seams, the needle's repeated arc and dive a pattern so easy to discern and comprehend.

But instead of explaining away the apparent contradictions, I have learned to simply make room for them, to believe it is possible that I was both of those girls at once, to understand that no life ever completely adds up. I remind myself that we all have complicated faces, that each of us is actually many people, that a life with loose ends is no less marvelous, no less saturated with meaning.

And sometimes I just give up. There are good days and bad days.

But that is precisely the point. Meaning does not pull me along in its powerful one-way train; it is, instead, something to sort through and sit with, something to find and then lose and then discover all over again.

It is also a fluid force, not at all immune to the context in which I try to grapple with it. I am not the little girl I wonder about — the fastidious tomboy, the fearless wallflower — though she still exists inside me. I write from this point in time, this location: in a house that has a family of squirrels scurrying frantically inside its walls, in front of a window with a view of pine trees whose bark turns almost pink as the sun sinks into the mountains. I do not see the trees, sometimes, though I look out that window often. I do not always hear the squirrels, though they scamper and chirp inside the bay just over my head. My gaze is turned inward; my ears are trained on catching the whisper of the past.

But on days when the woods look particularly gorgeous, I might remember that my childhood was filled with bright surprises and fresh breezes; on days when I feel inexplicably blue, irritated beyond all proportion by the noise of skittering rodents above me, those same years might transform, in my recollection, into a time of infinite sadness. I have faith, however, that these contradictions, too, get somehow folded in, blended, and balanced out as I sit at the computer and type, that my story is essentially the same each time — no matter how different — because it is constantly and consistently driven by the impulse to search and explore. What I come up with and eventually settle on will always be simultaneously right and not quite right, no matter how many times I adjust my emphasis, no matter what I include or weed out. This is the paradox of memory; it is its greatest magic.

Shadow Girl

Swallow

When I was seven years old, I decided — for no reason I can recollect — that before going to bed I had to eat a sheet of paper. Every night after my parents had tucked me in, I turned on the bedside lamp, climbed out of bed, and tore one piece of the stationery my aunt had given me for my birthday off the pad on my desk. The paper was pink, with cherry-colored lines, and at the top of each page was my name, capital letters, also in cherry, but with a little bit of sheen, and raised slightly, the way a scab provides the skin with texture. I could trace the letters with my eyes closed.

I bit off pieces and chewed, and the paper tasted terrible, but still, I enjoyed the ritual so much: working the tough paper inside my mouth, feeling it go soggy, my tongue sliding over the smooth gloss of the letters. And then the accomplishment of swallowing, finally, the pinkness of the paper going down deep, blending in with the pink I imagined my insides to be, and then dissolving. I would go to bed so satisfied, thinking of the shiny letters of my name, little cherry-colored bubbles floating through my body, lifting me, carrying me off, reflecting the sun, the moon, whatever I wanted.

"Delicious!" my mother said to me so often in those years, patting me a few times on the butt, or pulling me in for a hug. "I'd like to just eat you up!" And I knew in those moments, enveloped by her deep affection, her sweet gardenia perfume, that I could be devoured.

Where was she now, where was my father? Down the hall in their bedroom, watching TV in silence; downstairs with my brother, arguing about schoolwork — I didn't know. They were not a part of this. I was on my own, for once, my actions not directed by their silences, their words, the pain in their faces, not shaped by what they needed.

There I stood, in the middle of my room, eating paper, eating my name. All the furniture was color-coordinated, the books on my shelves were arranged in size order, sloping pleasingly from left to right, just the way I liked it. I was like a present, a parent's dream — teeth brushed, pajama top and bottom matching, toes wriggling on the shag rug, soft hair shining.

But this was not a present, this was something for me, something all about me: a girl consuming her own name, drawing nourishment from her self. And so it felt a little sneaky to me, not quite right — and yet, so essential, so urgent a task.

I marvel now at my ability to feed myself, to take such good care. I marvel at the sheer resourcefulness of the enterprise. But how desperate I was, to have to resort to these measures. How clear it must have been to me even then that there was no way to hold onto what was mine, to protect myself — from collapse, from compromise — to honor myself as something discrete and whole, to acknowledge that I was a being with borders, with boundaries, no way other than this: eating sheet after sheet of personalized stationery, consuming the letters of my name, burying them inside — the only safe place — closing my mouth tight, swallowing hard.

Family Tree

The straps of my dress were sliding off my shoulders, my cheeks were sunburnt to the color of red clay. I was three-and-a-half years old and I was with my parents and my brother, Danny, my aunt and uncle and grandparents. We were in Israel, planting a tree in a row of saplings. There were rows of saplings just like this one all around us, but behind them, way off in the distance, looking flat and inappropriate, like a stage backdrop someone forgot to change, was desert. The soil beneath us was pale, almost sandy. When we walked, our sandals kicked up little clouds.

I was too young to understand that planting trees in Israel was something Jewish American families had begun to do to help the reforestation effort: sending money from the U.S. and having a tree planted in their name, or, when they visited Israel, buying a tree and having the honor of planting it for themselves. I did not know that what we were doing, while it had the airy novelty of a trend, carried the symbolism of something much hardier and more longstanding — tradition, ritual: we were purchasing a young pine, our very own, and planting it next to the Bergmans', behind the Nussbaums', in front of the Silversteins', in the arid soil that was considered home ground, where it would grow despite the odds. We were re-creating the landscape; we were putting our roots down.

But while I could not define the gesture we were making or identify the specific symbolism, I could tell we were participating in something important, something larger than ourselves. I was part of a tableau: three generations assembled around a moment of meaning. The scene contained ceremony, which translated to me as solemnity, heaviness.

Danny seemed not to see things in the same way. He was seven and needed always to be on the move. He kept running away with the rusty shovel we had been given to dig our hole and had to be chased down the row of trees, my mother grabbing him by the hand, exasperated, and leading him back to us.

My father's knees cracked as he squatted down with the sapling in his hands. He carried it the way men carried the Torah when we went to *shul* every Saturday morning: delicately, gingerly, with a combination of love and awe. They wanted to hug it but also keep it at arm's length. He lowered the tree into the ground. The earth ball, swaddled in burlap, fit snugly inside the hole.

My father had planned the outing; he was in charge of this activity. He led our two-week visit to the Holy Land, his enthusiasm like a current carrying us all along.

Maybe at night in their hotel room, after Danny and I had gone to sleep, my parents argued about what was planned for the next day, my mother lobbying for a relaxing morning in front of the pool, my father pushing for a tour of some ancient ruins. But maybe the strife didn't come until later. I like to think there was a period, in the beginning, when things worked between them. I like to think there was a period during which I viewed them as a single entity, and loved them that way.

So there was my mother, her hand resting on my father's shoulder as he deposited the tree into the earth: a reassuring touch, not a demand. I have put her there.

Everyone took turns covering up the earth ball, burying the sapling's roots, rearranging the soil around them with the shovel.

"Here, Debbie," my father said. "Do you want to help?" He held up the shovel. "Come on, we'll do it together."

My mother and father were looking at me, smiling with their mouths closed, and the air was dry and hot. The whole landscape seemed silent and still, except for a fly buzzing somewhere behind my back.

But the moment felt too loaded with significance. Too much rested on my reply; it was an acceptance of a kind of burden. There was expectation, somehow; there was the terrible push of promise. I felt paralyzed by what was required of me; I felt trapped.

And suddenly I felt sorry for the sapling too: a baby, as vulnerable as I, the whole heavy future resting on its delicate branches, those who nurtured it — with gentle shovelfuls of dirt and, later, with water from a snaking green hose — also weighing it down, laying upon it all the heft of their love and hope. What a predicament.

There was a pressure deep inside of me, and I wanted to turn and find the buzzing sound, I wanted to follow the fly on its wild path, spin off into space, go anywhere. I wanted to erase that spot, that place and time, close my eyes and pull away into a deep blue nothing, vanish.

I did not know what I wanted.

I looked at my father and shook my head no, no; I would not help shovel the dirt. I turned away from the sapling and pressed my face into his neck; my tears puddled up in the dip behind his collarbone.

Why is this, of all things, my first memory? Is it the picture in the family album I used to flip through as a child that has fixed the incident so vividly in my mind: me in my stiff kibbutznik hat, my dress a simple triangle, my tiny hand resting on my father's shoulder as he squats down with the tree?

Perhaps. But there were so many pictures from that trip, so many other trips: so many possible beginnings. And yet this is the image that has always animated itself before my eyes when I look through those pictures, brought me back to a real moment in time. While other memories slipped away, gone for good, the details of this incident only sharpened over the years, the colors of the day grew more vivid. It was a memory that meant something, etched into my brain because of everything that followed: emblematic, a beginning arrived at retroactively.

This, then, is how my life started: with ambivalence, confusion; with me turning from the shovel's angled blade, from the sapling; with me turning from the demands and expectation of family, and then, with tears in my eyes, turning back again for sustenance, for refuge.

No one could understand why I was crying. My mother felt my forehead for evidence of a fever. My aunt and grandmother leaned their heads in together, whispering. I could not explain to them why I was so sad. I did not have the language to express myself, or the heart. I swallowed and blinked up at them, dark figures circled around the baby tree, my tears turning the sun behind them into a complicated jewel.

Secret Body

There were moments when I was curious, satisfied, intent on my own exploration, untroubled, when I was a girl who knew how to search the world, make discoveries, rejoice. That, too, is a part of the way things were. I insist.

There was a backyard to run through; there was a place where the bushes that bordered our property thinned out at the bottom, and in the summertime I could crawl inside and lie on my back in the dirt. Tiny leaves, dark green and eye-shaped, filled the safe blue sky above my head like stars.

One day a baby bird fell out of that sky and broke its wing against the ground, but we cared for it and helped it heal. My father put the bird in a cardboard box beneath the maple tree, and Danny and I took turns feeding it worms we had dug up, and occasionally the mother bird came by for visits, perching expertly on the thin edge of the box. A week later the box was empty; the bird had flown away.

Still, even these pleasant memories darken as I handle them, like a photograph improperly fixed. I seem inevitably to find the underbelly of each moment, and then I can't figure out where to place the emphasis, where the true essence of my experience lay. Was it the bird's flight that caught me, did I ride on its wings into the sky? Or was it the empty box below, lined with parched, browning grass and littered with the bird's own excrement, which crumbled when I poked it with a stick?

One Sunday afternoon when I was four, I was playing on the swing set with my friend Melanie Jacobs. We didn't actually swing on the swings anymore — that was something we had gotten bored of months ago. Our new game was to climb the swing set and then stand on top of the crossbars at either end, where the *A* was, so we could reach the grapes that were growing at the edge of the yard, grabbing for them with one hand, holding onto one of the poles with the other. The grapes didn't taste very good — they were tart and hard, you couldn't even smush them between your fingers — but we liked picking them anyway. We staged contests — who could do the neatest job peeling the skins off, who could throw them farthest across the lawn. We tried to find the biggest one, the skinniest one, the funniest-looking one.

I saw some grapes that looked particularly plump higher up on the vine. But I couldn't get to them just by standing on the crossbar and reaching out, so I started to shimmy up the outside of the *A*, my knees pressing against the pole and holding me in place until I pushed myself up a little farther, grabbed a little higher with my hands. Suddenly, there was a great squeeze and release right between my legs, like a beautiful, strong hand quickly opening and closing. I didn't know what was happening. It was like falling into the softest space, spreading out in all directions, a stretch that was simultaneously luxurious and violent. My toes curled inside my sandals. I felt so warm and loose I thought I might have peed, but when I touched my Danskin shorts, everything was dry.

At the top of the swing set, I forgot about the grapes that I had climbed up for. I just slid down to the crossbar and climbed right back up again, hoping the same thing — whatever in the world it was — would happen once more. Sure enough, it did.

"Melanie," I said. "Try this. It feels really good right here." I stuck my hand between my legs and clamped my thighs around it.

Melanie cocked her head and raised one eyebrow. She wasn't sure what to think. Melanie became a math whiz in elementary school and eventually grew up to be a doctor; already, she needed science, hard data, to understand. I could not offer her that.

"C'mon," I said. "Just try it." She didn't exactly believe me, but she climbed up on her end of the swing set anyway. She was skeptical but also loyal. Just the other day in kindergarten she had pointed out that because I was the closest to five years old of anyone in the class, everyone else should listen to me.

She slid right back down and shrugged her shoulders. "I didn't feel anything."

"Maybe you're not doing it right," I told her. "Try again." This time I watched carefully to make sure she was moving exactly the way I was. I wanted so much for her to know what had just happened to me, to have her body do the same dance. I could already picture the afternoon ahead of us, the endless climbing and sliding, the great surge over and over, the experience uniting us in this little section of the yard while my parents wandered around indoors doing grown-up things, the September sun sending out long fingers of light, tingeing everything with gold.

Melanie and I were always finding ways to exclude the rest of the world; we were always scheming, telling each other secrets, inventing intimacies that had to be carefully safeguarded. Later on that year, we started to speak Ubby-Dubby, which we learned from watching *Zoom!* on TV, so quickly that no one else knew what we were talking about. "Girls!" my mother would say, shaking her head and blinking her eyes quickly in mock disbelief, as though she couldn't quite trust her ears. "Since when do you two know French? Could someone please translate for me?" In first grade we spent whole afternoons lying on my bed dreaming up fantasies in which our Hebrew teacher, Mrs. Atzmon, rescued us from various dangers: a falling plane, a maple tree with claws, a toilet that sucked you in when you sat down. In second grade we began to create our own language — one in which one English word substituted for another — writing down our vocabulary on duplicate lists that we folded up stamp-size and carried around with us at all times. "Did you see your mother's Virginia?" one of us would say, and we would both break down laughing. "Her brakes are huge!" It was not hard to crack the code, but we felt immune to adult understanding anyway.

Melanie climbed up again, just the way I did, but nothing happened, except that on the way down, she slid too fast, her dress got bunched up around her waist, and she burned the insides of her thighs.

"Oww," she said, and lifted her dress up to show me the red marks. Then she turned back to the grapevines.

But I gave up on the grapes and spent the rest of the afternoon climbing the three-foot stretch of pole and sliding back down. Now there was a divide between us, a bit of space, though there was also great companionship. She was still my Melanie, the one whose hand I would reach for when we lined up double file for recess at school the next day, the one who would be over at my house again the next weekend, but it seemed as though when I looked at her now at the other end of the swing set, her frizzy hair trained into two stiff braids, I was looking *back* at her, from a new place, exciting but also solitary. She could not meet me there, and I could not even adequately explain its terrain.

We talked a little bit, but mostly we stayed busy with our individual projects. Sometimes Melanie stopped to show me a particularly interesting grape.

"Look at *this* one," she said, her droopy brown eyes wide with delight at the bounty of the observable world. She held each one in her outstretched palm so I could see and then tossed it into the bushes behind her with a quick jerk. An odd-looking, pear-shaped grape; a baby grape, the size of a pearl earring; a grape she had peeled with such care that the flesh was still intact — smooth, slick, flawless.

Melanie's parents came to pick her up at the end of the day. "Real characters," my mother was always saying about them. "It's like they're caught in the fifties." And it's true there was something old-fashioned, almost black-and-white about them; going to their house was like walking into one of the TV shows on channel 9. Mr. Jacobs smoked a pipe and put on a brim hat whenever he left the house; his dark eyes glistened against his ashen skin. Mrs. Jacobs wore pedal pushers and flats and always spoke in careful whispers, like a librarian. She breathed into the *w* at the beginning of words. "*Hwhen* do you think you'll be over next?" she would ask me. And, "*Hwhy* don't you use the powder room before you leave?" Their house was dimly lit; they wore only the darkest colors.

I stood on the front steps of our house with my father, waving good-bye as they all pulled out of the driveway in their boxy black car, Melanie in the back seat, her nose pressed against the glass.

"Dad," I said, tugging on my father's fingers to get his attention. "You know what happened before?"

He gave one last wave and then turned to me. "No," he said. "Tell me what happened."

"When I climbed up the side of the swing set, it felt good right here." With my other hand, I showed him.

His eyes lost focus; he looked suddenly distracted. "Hmmm . . . ?" he said, and turned back toward Melanie's car, now on its way down the road. "Let's go inside and see what Mom's doing, okay?"

I wonder what went through my father's mind in the moment after I shared my surprise with him; I try to imagine the tumble of thought and feeling that led him to respond in the way that he did. What can a father possibly say to his daughter when she delivers this kind of news, the little girl whom he has sat on his lap for endless hours, whose body he has sponged during fever, whose bottom he has spanked when she has misbehaved? The girl he knows will someday be a woman, but whom he cannot in his heart admit will be anything other than the child before him: shining hair, smooth legs that still show a trace of baby pudge around the knees, square teeth that line up like tiny tiles, a smile that resembles his own? How jarring that I would present him with such clear evidence of the future.

And I wonder what kind of murky discomfort this evidence stirred up in him, darkening his devotion with the shadow of something else, tainting the kiss he had delivered tucking me in the night before.

But what did I know, as a little girl? I knew this: My father had not ever been this way before — so distant, preoccupied. I had been accustomed to sharing everything with him, but things were different this time. Somewhere beneath thought, I made the connection, I drew conclusions: my words had created a gulf between us; what I told him pushed him away. I realized it was dangerous and powerful, this thing that had blossomed inside me on the swing set; it could make my father retreat from me, turn his eyes away from mine, unlock the gaze that often held us.

We went inside and there was my mother, in the kitchen, scrubbing the countertop, scraping grime out of the crack between the sink and the Formica. An instinct rose up in me. It told me to keep her away from this experience; it told me this was not something she would understand.

I had sat on her bed so many times and watched her prepare for an evening out with my father, examining herself in the mirror, throwing her shoulders back and telling herself she really had to work on her posture. She fixed her hair, training her cowlicks into place with a hairdryer and a few quick yanks with a circular brush. She applied her lipstick, the pressure of the tube pushing her upper lip past her gum, first on one side, then the other, and then dragging her lower lip down. Her mouth turned the color of dried blood; there was violence in the gesture.

And I had watched her turn down the thrill of plunging into a chilly pond, eating a slice of flourless chocolate cake, letting a golden retriever's tongue slide across her face, all pink wet muscle. I had watched her refuse to yield to the push of my father's strong hands working the knots in her back. "Too hard, Ed," she told him, tensing up, then shrugging him off. "That hurts."

She was already on her way to becoming the woman I would know when I was in high school, her tiny, fat-free body racked with mysterious aches, an independent presence to do cautious battle with, to dread. Even the endless pampering she would submit to, which masqueraded as appreciation, sprang from a kind of fearful respect: who knew what else might go wrong without the massages, without the creams lined up against the vanity mirror?

Through my mother I would eventually learn that the body was not a storehouse of delightful surprises, but just messy flesh: a nuisance, an interference, something to get past. I would learn that the body was not an instrument of pleasure and connection — to oneself, to the great sensual world — but the locus of pain and disappointment.

What happened on the swing set — it was a moment that made me more fully myself: a child of my parents, a friend, but also just me, a girl in a body that knew how to respond. I had the sense of hunkering down, stripping away what did not matter, drawing in closer to the dull, knobby blades that were my bones, hearing more loudly the thump of my heart, which told me who I really was.

I also had the sense of aloneness. The experience meant a piece of independence, a girl testing out her own body's responses. But it also confused my father and put some distance between us; it left my mother behind.

I did not let anyone else know about my discovery; I guarded it within the walls of my body. It developed as a secret, a private quest for pleasure, the muscles wrenching themselves, over and over, into intense, unspoken joy.

I looked for poles everywhere; I climbed whatever I could. Walking into a furniture store with my mother one day, I felt a rush of excitement when I spotted a coffee table with legs that extended past the glass surface: six inches of metal for me to rub myself against. She and I were always going to furniture stores. My mother was forever in the midst of some zealous redecorating plan. She had gotten business cards made up that said she was an interior decorator, so she could get a decorator's discount on whatever she purchased. Now, as she headed up to the front of the store to find a salesperson, I saw her reaching into her pocketbook to pull out a card. We both had our deceptions.

I hung back, and when she was safely out of view, I rushed over to the coffee table. I plunked myself down against the pointy leg — but too hastily, sloppily; it jabbed into the most tender part of me and made it sting. I was so sore I had to leave myself alone for a couple of days.

But there were plenty of other things that gave me better success — the picket fence in my friend Diana's backyard, the stanchions that held up the net at the tennis court where my mother played on Tuesday afternoons, the stop signs and parking meters all over downtown, where she and I ran errands. So that nobody would know what I was doing, I concentrated on keeping my face serene, my features smooth, the surface of my being looking completely relaxed while below, deep inside, I was all wild spasms.

The jungle gym at school, with its network of metal poles stretching up into the sky, took on new importance for me. All through recess I climbed up and slid back down, not wanting to join in the games that were going on around me — boys chasing girls, girls chasing boys, the occasional kiss planted hard on the lips, followed by a squeal. The chatter around me became muffled, faded out, as though I were listening to echoes instead of the real thing.

Sometimes it happened even without a pole to climb. Watching professional wrestling, for example: the wrestlers in their brightly colored tights throwing each other around in the ring, their hair flowing past their shoulders, their wide belts, with flashy buckles as big as plates, severing them in two. They all had the look of having once been in top shape; their bodies somehow managed to retain the memory of sharply angled silhouettes, while the muscles themselves had begun to go slack, the flesh rippling from the impact of the opponent's blow. And then there were the professional bodybuilders — well-muscled bodies gone too huge and hard, veins as thick as tree roots pushing through dark, oiled skin, the poses that turned the back into a pair of wings unfolding and collapsing, the stomach into rungs of a ladder.

They were opposite extremes, but they were also different faces of the same phenomenon. In either case, I knew, on some level, that what I was watching was performance; I had a sense that it was all slightly obscene, that these were parodies of men, not quite the real thing. But at the time I did not wonder why these spectacles — the men preening, histrionic, laughable, even desperate — affected me so.

Perhaps it was the combination of the erotic and the cartoonish: the very fact that these men were there — flexing, grunting, hurting each other, outdoing each other (for me?) — touching something already old in me, pulling an ancient trigger, while the exaggerated displays of male power appealed to all that was childish, unsubtle. My brain was wired to receive certain signals, my muscles were primed to respond. And yet I was still a girl, a four-year-old who hoped that someday Mr. Clean would emerge from the bottle under the kitchen sink so I could stroke the shiny dome of his head, who believed in the Pillsbury doughboy and nagged my mother to buy just one box of biscuits at the supermarket so he would come out and play with me on the kitchen counter at home. I longed to press my finger into the soft white flesh of his belly.

One night not long after the moment on the swing set, I discovered something else. I was lying in bed unable to sleep, tossing and flipping and rearranging my pillow. At one point I was lying with the pillow under me lengthwise and I decided to experiment: I rolled it up, placed my hands underneath it for additional pressure. I slowly wriggled my way up to the headboard. It seemed to work at least as well as any hard metal pole. I closed my eyes and my bed became a whole planet, tilting this way and that.

Eventually the pillow replaced everything else — it was always there, always warm, and my bedroom was a private place. Afterward, I could drift off to sleep. Up and down I went, night after night, trying to keep myself as quiet as possible, even though sometimes I wanted to let out a big sigh or groan, so my parents wouldn't hear me down the hall and find out what I'd been up to.

Over time, what I did with my pillow began to feel like a special power, a cherished, unique gift hidden inside me, protected. It had been happening for so long in private I couldn't imagine anyone else knowing anything about it. Under the covers at night, I drew on that power. My secret body took over. The movements were my own invention, and I was the first girl in the world.

It took no time at all — a couple of minutes at most — and I could have done it a handful of times every night before falling asleep if I wanted to. But I always held back, rationing — never allowing myself more than two of these special moments (how odd that I never gave them a name) each night. I believed I had been born with a limited number, and — with my whole life ahead of me — I didn't want to use them all up.

Perhaps the restriction I imposed on myself is evidence of a child's need for structure, her dependence on limits. It was a careful meting out of pleasure — much like the two-cookie limit, the half-hour of TV per night, bedtime at eight-thirty, no exceptions. I was being my own parent.

Being my own parent: yes, here was my mother's influence. I brought her back to me after all, I included her. She was there checking up on me, perching to examine my broken wing, my fall from control into the softness of orgasm, a dirty place. She would help me heal. The rationing was a way of keeping desire from getting completely out of hand; it was a way of preventing the imagined disaster that would befall me if I didn't keep myself in check: a numbness between my legs, the loss of physical joy. Already, in my mind, the quest for sensual experience had to be reined in with discipline, was associated with punishment, came tinged with the smell of recklessness, of greed.

Escher's Hands

I.

y mother was standing at the kitchen counter, talking to someone on the phone, her head tipped to the right, squeezing the receiver against her shoulder. She was writing down directions on a pad.

"Get off at what exit?" she said. Then, "Yah, okay . . . okay."

Her left hand was wedged into the back pocket of her jeans, her elbow stuck out behind her. I reached up and pulled her hand out. It hung down right at my eye level. I spread her fingers apart, closed my fist around each one. The skin was so soft, it seemed to be on the verge of dissolving; she kept a bottle of Neutrogena on the windowsill above the kitchen sink and pumped out a few squirts every time she washed her hands or did the dishes. The flesh on the rest of her body was smooth and taut, but her hands were wrinkled and always looked swollen. If I tugged on her wedding ring, which was actually four plain, separate bands — one for each of the mothers of Israel — it stopped at her knuckle and refused to go any farther. The nails were shaped in careful curves that were almost clear; I held her hand up toward the fluorescent bulb on the ceiling and saw light coming through at the tips of her fingers.

I turned her palm out toward me, traced the heavy lines that crossed it with my forefinger. Looking up, I could see a path from her hand all the way up her arm and into her body, the place where she understood things, the place where she knew.

I began to whisper into her palm, certain the words would travel along that path, that her body would hear me. "Mom," I said. "I have a question."

I chose her palm rather than the back of her hand because the underside of the hand was openness, the part that received, that accepted sensation: my mother's hand pressed against my forehead, palm side down, to check for fever, her hands cupping her eyes as she said a prayer after lighting candles every Friday night, our palms facing each other as we waved good-bye at nursery school.

"Right turn after the second traffic light," she was saying. "Hmm-hmm."

"Mom," I continued. My breath heated up her palm, moistened it, the deep crevices in her skin collected the sounds I was making. "Mom, I want to know, can I have noodles and cottage cheese for dinner, please?"

I looked up and waited for her to nod her head yes.

"Okay," my mother said, and for a split second I thought she was talking to me. "So we'll see you on Sunday then. Right. Bye."

After she hung up the phone, my mother explained to me that she couldn't hear through her hand, that hands didn't hear things, only ears did. I understood what she had told me — of course, ears are for hearing, silly, not hands! — but it didn't make sense to me. I still couldn't believe that my words did not reach her, there was such a clear path between our bodies.

II.

One day while my mother was taking a nap, I snuck into her bedroom and grabbed her clothes from the armchair near her bed, where she had tossed them in a heap. I brought the bundle into my room and put it all on over what I was already wearing. First, the blue jeans, which were so big I had to stand with my legs spread out, cowboy-style, to keep them from dropping down to my ankles. Then her fuzzy red sweater, the cowl touching the middle of my chest, the waist hanging to my knees. I got confused and put her bra on over the sweater, managing to loop one of the hooks into one of the eyes in front and then twisting the whole thing around to the back, just as I had seen her do. I threaded my arms through the straps and held my shoulders up high so the straps didn't fall.

Then I stepped into her light blue wedge slippers and waddled around the room for a couple of minutes, saying, "Debbie, it's time for you to wake up. C'mon, kiddo, let's go. Debbie, it's time for you to get dressed. We'll make finger puppets today, we'll read *All of a Kind Family*."

But when I caught sight of myself in the three-paneled mirror on my dresser, I was horrified. Nothing looked right. The bra cups were wrinkled, collapsed like a couple of rotten vegetables. They sagged at my belly, in full view. I had put my mother on inside out, I had ruined her. I quickly peeled the clothes off my body and put them back onto the armchair by her bed.

After my mother woke up from her nap, I confessed to her what I had done. I worried she would be angry at me for taking her clothing without asking — for acting before telling her first — but I could not carry the secret inside of me. I could not betray her.

But my mother was not bothered; in fact, she was amused. The one thing that upset her was that I had worn her slippers. She worried I might catch the fungus that had turned the toenails on her right foot into bumpy yellow rocks that she had to file down with a pumice stone in order to fit comfortably into her shoe.

And then it seemed okay, what I had done; it wasn't such a bad thing after all.

Still, I felt guilty. I felt I had done damage; I felt a private terror I could not communicate. I had put the bra on over the red sweater, I had jumbled the image of my mother. It was as though I had discovered something terrible about her: that she was always merely a collection of fragile layers that might easily, even unwittingly, be disturbed.

III.

We were about to go to the airport to pick up my grandparents. My mother told me to sit on the toilet before we left. She said it was a long drive, and we certainly didn't want to be stopping on the way. But I didn't have to go to the bathroom at all. When I pressed on my belly it felt empty. Besides, I was wearing my new gingham jumper, with my white blouse perfectly smoothed out and tucked into my underpants in exactly the right way, and I didn't want to mess anything up. I was fussy about my clothing: I refused to go to bed once when a babysitter dressed me in mismatched pajamas; the shoes in my closet were always all lined up side by side. This fussiness — this strong need for things to be in their place — was one of the things my mother loved about me; or perhaps it was merely the order it usually generated that pleased her so.

I told her I didn't have to go.

"Just try," she said.

"I don't want to."

"Just try," she said again, taking me by the hand. "Come on, we'll tuck your blouse in again when you're done. It'll be just the same as before."

She led me down the hall to the bathroom. I stomped my feet with each step, but mostly for show. I was an obedient child, not one for serious fits; she didn't have to do any tugging.

I pulled my underpants down and the fabric of my blouse sprang out in all directions. I hiked my dress up around my chest and watched it bunch up and wrinkle, the gingham pattern collapsed in on itself, a jumble of broken squares and odd angles. This was terrible.

I sat down on the toilet bowl. Nothing. I wriggled my toes, I swung my feet. Still nothing. My mother leaned against the sink and looked at me.

"Psshhh," she said.

And suddenly I was peeing, as though she had just reached her hand far inside of me and found her way to a faucet I didn't even know about, opening it up with a quick turn of the wrist and then retreating.

"See?" she said, smiling.

When we got to the airport, I had to go again. All the excitement, my mother said. We headed off to the public bathroom. She pushed open the door to the nearest stall with her elbow, wrinkled her nose, and whispered, "*Pfuey teifl!* Who knows what kind of germs are floating around?"

I didn't mind undressing now, since she hadn't tucked in my blouse very well after I peed at home. There was the chance that she would do a better job this time.

We locked ourselves in a precarious embrace. It was a routine I knew well, my mother grabbing me under the thighs and lifting me off the ground while I hooked my hands over her shoulders, so that she was holding me a good foot above the toilet and I was touching nothing, trying my best not to splatter despite the way she shook from the strain.

Afterward, I stuck my hands under the faucet and she pumped soap from the dispenser.

"Lucky thing," she said, and I could tell she was talking more to herself than to me. "Most of these places don't even have soap." She looked at my reflection in the mirror. "Delicious," she said, straightening the collar of my shirt, which she had tucked in just fine this time around. Then she led me back out the door and, even though I was wearing sandals, instructed me to walk on my heels so I didn't get athlete's foot.

IV.

On TV there was a show with cowboys and Indians. The Indians hooted and acted underhanded, sneaking up on the cowboys when they weren't prepared, shooting arrows into their backs while they were sitting around the campfire at night. The cowboys fought nobly, shooting the Indians in the chest with guns during full-fledged, daytime battles, when they charged each other on horseback. The horses' rumps were as round and polished as apples. The Indians fell backward off their horses and hit the ground. My brother whooped with delight, urging the cowboys on.

Occasionally, a stray bullet or arrow would hit one of the horses. The horse reared up, throwing its rider, and then staggered to the ground. When this happened, I began to wail. I could take all the warfare — in fact, the sight of dying cowboys and Indians hardly interested me — but I could not take the dying horses.

My mother came running into the room, but when she saw what was going on, her face closed up.

"Quiet," she said. "It's just a show." She said this not to soothe me, but simply to get me to stop. There was anger running just below the sound of her words, a resentment she did not try to conceal. Unless I was physically ill, my tears always seemed to undo her in this way, shattering her very skin, cracking the floor of the world on which she normally tread so that she was forced to scramble for firm ground.

In my defense I pointed to the horse on the screen, lying on its side, perfectly still.

"Debbie," she said. "That's no reason to cry."

"Why?" I asked her, my question fusing into another long wail, though at this point I was no longer crying only about the horse. I was also crying because of what I had done to her, the damage my grief had caused.

"Because it's a horse on a TV show," she told me. "That's it. That's all it is." She walked across the carpeted floor and reached to turn off the TV.

"Hey, wait a minute!" Danny yelled, and then stuck his tongue out at me, annoyed that the commotion I caused had interrupted his show.

My mother punched in the knob on the TV with her fist. A spark flew off her hand with a small, sharp click.

"Ach!" she said, pulling back quickly at the electric shock. She stood there for a moment, eyes wide, staring at her fingers as though they had betrayed her by catching the current of electricity, exposing her to the world's tiny sparks of pain. Then she quickly left the room.

V.

My mother and I were at the beach. It was crowded, and I was disappointed. I had hoped there would be a long stretch of sand on either side of us, a dark-haired duo clumped together like a beauty mark on a smooth, gigantic thigh.

I wanted to go in the water, but even though I could swim just fine, I was not allowed without my mother, who wasn't hot enough yet to get wet. Even on a sticky day like this — we had heard on the radio that it was 90 degrees, and there was hardly a breeze, even at the ocean — she didn't break a sweat.

I lay there on my back, humming to myself, making designs in the sand with my fingers, digging my feet way down where it was cool, waiting. My mother flipped through her *Architectural Digest*, sighing from time to time: there was so much that she wanted. A couple of boys raced each other to the water, kicking sand onto my corner of the blanket by mistake. I crawled to the edge and tried to wipe the blanket clean, but my weight shifted the small mounds underneath and the sand only slid more to the center.

When she was finally ready, my mother walked with me to the shoreline. I splashed in right away, but she stopped when the water was just up to her thighs. She stood there for a while with her hands on her hips, knees locked, scanning the horizon. Suddenly she dunked into the water, but only up to her neck; she didn't want to have to wash her hair again that night. I grabbed onto her shoulders, slid my fingers into the deep grooves her bra straps had created over the years. How soft and yielding she was: her skin recording the pressure of her clothing, her hair flattened out each morning by sleep, her face sliced with a new collection of red creases from her pillowcase.

I wrapped my legs around her hips. One leg brushed against the mole at the base of her back, a brownish pebble, and I wondered why it didn't ever fall off, it seemed to be attached so tenuously. After twirling me in circles and bobbing me up and down, my mother peeled off my arms and legs and I began to float away.

I practiced the crawl I had learned at day camp while she did a few strokes of her own, slapping her arms against the surface of the water, cupping her hands hard, as though she was grabbing for something that kept disappearing.

VI.

Everything about her was stiff, awkward. The way she smiled — her lips pulled back far into her cheeks, her mouth still closed — as if someone had come up to her and pushed her face into that position against her will. The way she shook hands, thrusting her forearm out in a broad, overeager jerk. The way she drew her shoulders back at the dinner table, trying to sit up straight, overcompensating so that her back arched and her chest pressed forward. The way she walked, like a marionette, in an attempt to move with a stride that conveyed assurance. Only when she was upset did she shed her enamel casing, her arms hanging down at precisely the right angle, her feet the perfect distance apart. It was as though her body was trying to learn a second language — the language of unending joy, of unflappable self-confidence — but had lived too long with the first ever to become close to fluent. Every gesture was self-conscious, a staged articulation.

Part of her knew it was a lost cause, she was trapped in her own slope-shouldered sadness. So she directed her energy toward me. It was not that I was a particularly melancholy child or especially lacking in self-esteem; it was that my very presence suggested to her this possibility, the potential for all the deep wounds that were her own. Maybe she could catch me early enough to train my shoulders into the posture of social success, arrange my chin at such a height that I would appear nearly regal.

She was always telling me to sit up straight, hold my head up high, look people right in the eye when I was talking to them. She told me the world would not take notice of me otherwise. She told me to speak up. She told me to smile. She told me no one likes a sourpuss. When I beamed at her as I had learned, somehow, to do, giving her what was required, she smiled back, her own pain finally erased.

VII.

It was a late summer morning, school hadn't started yet, and there was life in my room. I was writing in my journal, I was daydreaming about a boy with bright green eyes and olive skin, I was lying on my back and looking at the daisies on my ceiling. Their petals, outlined in blue, seemed to shimmer and blink. My mind soared and dipped. There were worlds spinning lazily through my head. I watched them come and go.

The stairs creaked; my mother was on her way up.

"Come on out," she said, poking her head in through the door. She had been in the backyard, suntanning. Her nose and cheeks were already brown. "It's a beautiful day. It's not healthy to be indoors all the time."

She started out solicitous, but when I didn't hop off the bed and hurry out the door, her voice turned clipped, agitated. "This is no way to spend a morning, alone like this, in your room. Let's go." She clapped her hands together once, the way you would to get a distracted dog interested in coming. My solitude frightened her, my interior life was a choice, a betrayal, a wall she could not break through.

I didn't say anything. I was shut down by my anger, suddenly exhausted.

"Okay, Deb," she told me, her face registering an eerie combination of frustration and cheer. "I'll see you outside in a few minutes then!" As she turned to go, I noticed the backs of her legs were stamped with red diamonds from the lounge chair in the backyard.

I was perfectly content to be lying there thinking, while the breeze rustled the leaves of the maple tree outside my window and then swept across my bare feet, to be letting my thoughts drop in and flutter off like sparrows. I didn't want to leave that room.

But it felt different now, as though some invisible membrane that surrounded me — as delicate as the skin of a jellyfish or a bubble-gum bubble — had been punctured, ruined. The atmosphere was raw, the space no longer my own dreamy world, but just my bedroom, which had not changed since I was five, full of ugly flower prints in the brashest yellows and greens.

I was thirteen years old. It was around this time that I began to imagine my whole body in red — an organ vulnerable and aching, a wound she kept pressing herself into.

Many years later I would begin cutting my arms with a kitchen knife, parallel slices, evenly spaced. This was how I had come to know myself, and also to find solace: through intrusion, a painful break in the surface. I felt soothed then, safe, the edges bleeding in a familiar way, the thin slices on my forearm rungs of a rescue ladder I was offering myself.

VIII.

My mother was sitting on the couch in the den, reading this week's library book, the plastic cover crinkling whenever she adjusted her legs. She loved to read books like this one, thick sagas that followed European immigrants to the New World, where they build fortunes, have affairs, produce children and grandchildren and great-grandchildren. The book sat flat in her lap, her head bent over it at an awful angle, her

chin almost tucked into her chest. She always read folded into this unnatural position. In bed at night, while my father slept or watched TV,
she lay flat on her back and rested the book on her stomach, her head
propped up, pushed too far forward, on three pillows.

I was sixteen years old and I could have been anywhere — in my
room alone, at the movies, on a train to New York City to see a
friend — but I was there on the couch behind my mother. I was on my
knees, with my heels tucked into my butt; kneeling gave me a better
vantage point. As my mother read, I combed through her hair with my
fingers, seeking out the flaky dry patches on her scalp, and scratching
the dandruff off with my fingernails. I moved methodically across her
head, parting her hair in small sections until I found my bounty. The
condition was so bad her scalp actually seemed thicker in those spots.
Big flakes fell out, wide but incredibly thin, the way the moon looks
when it's just risen into a daytime sky.

I could not explain why I did this, except to say that it provided me
with an almost sleepy kind of relief.

How wholly attentive I was, the world around me shut out, everything gone except the back of my mother's head. There was the faintly
oily smell of her hair, the tarry smell from the special shampoo she got
from the dermatologist. There was her scalp, white as a mushroom,
the mole at the base of her neck, the flakes collecting on her shoulders.

But how hurtful I was, too, erasing her, layer by layer, cell by cell.
There was anger in the gesture, an impulse toward destruction in the
way I scraped and scraped, peeling away the chunks of her body, until
there were raw patches, until she finally said, "Ow, that's enough."

Instead of stopping, I just flattened the hair down in that spot and
moved on to another section. Finally she grabbed my hand from her
head and pinned it down on the couch by her side. She stroked my
fingers absentmindedly with her thumb while she read.

She passed over the tough rinds of my cuticles and began to pick
at them with her thumbnail. The hardened skin chipped away in tiny
clicks.

She turned another page. I looked out the window.

We had been this way for so long it was impossible to live differ-
ently. There was a balance we could not undo, a symmetry we could
not break free of, like Escher's hands, each with a pencil poised between thumb and forefinger, rising up from the page, fist tight, drawing the other into existence.

In Place

The four of us were crowded into the upstairs bathroom, looking at the toilet with great interest and concern. Danny had called my parents in there, and I had followed them to see what all the fuss was about. It was something I did — trail behind to watch the drama unfold, present but not really participating: an audience. Often things ended badly, with loud voices and tears and the air in the room tight with rage, and yet I could not remove myself from the scene or shut it out. The worse things got, the more I was pulled in, the way I would turn back to stare at a squashed raccoon on the side of the road as we whizzed by it in the car, my gaze drawn to the pile of oozing fur, to the prospect of something terrifying and repulsive.

"The toilet won't flush," Danny announced to my parents, sounding vaguely alarmed. "See, watch what happens."

He reached to push down the lever, and my parents both lunged out to divert his hand.

"No, don't!" they cried in unison.

The water level was already dangerously high; one more flush could have sent it over the rim. At the bottom of the bowl, tendrils of white toilet paper moved around in gentle waves like underwater plant life, refusing to be sucked down.

We had been living in that house for two years, and up until that evening the pipes had been reliable, flushing mightily, carrying away waste, doing what they were supposed to do. Things operated smoothly; we had efficiency, tidiness, we ran a tight ship. But now something had gone wrong; there was badness lurking just out of view, the threat of overflow, of stench and mess. The problem was making everyone a little agitated.

The wrinkles deepened in my father's face; my mother said, "Oh, dear; oh, dear," and blew air against her bottom lip; I stood behind them, feeling the nerves in my body begin to ripple and flex.

My father told Danny to get the plunger from the basement, not looking at him while he talked but instead keeping his eye on the toilet, as though the situation might worsen of its own accord without this kind of vigilance.

Perhaps Danny felt responsible for what had happened, his own waste creating such chaos. Perhaps his shame made him defensive, so that he misinterpreted the edge in my father's voice as anger, could not tolerate the cloak of blame he believed was being placed upon him. Perhaps he was merely having a bad day. In any case, he bridled at my father's instructions.

"No," he said. "Why should I have to get it?"

"Because I'm asking you to get it, that's why."

Then my mother chimed in. "Danny," she said, "we really need the plunger. Could you please just go downstairs and get it?"

"No," Danny said again, his voice climbing, tears squeezing out of the corners of his eyes. "Why can't you do it?" He was nine years old and still cried easily.

My mother was suddenly crying too. "Ed," she said, "I can't take this. I just want to scream!" She held her hands up near her temples and shook them, a stagy move, her fingers splayed and arched like claws, as though she were on the verge of tearing her hair out in big clumps.

My father yelled at Danny, my mother cried some more, Danny bounced around the room on his toes like a boxer ready to strike, shouting, "No! You do it, you do it!" The three of them continued this way, each gesture or outburst an amplification of the one before, a refinement, a kind of zeroing in, as though they were practicing and practicing, everything getting streamlined, sped up, distilled into a shorthand version of what they really meant, an elliptical language of anger and frustration.

By now I had removed myself from the hot center of things, crossing the threshold from the pink octagonal tiles in the bathroom to the field of beige carpet in the hallway, neutral territory. I could still see and hear everything, but from where I stood it was all toned down just a notch, a little bit muted. It was safer.

They were so stuck, the three of them, like characters in a fairy tale frozen by the curse of an evil witch, and as I watched them argue, my fingers began to tingle with the thought of breaking the spell.

I quietly left them, went downstairs, and then downstairs again, and retrieved the plunger from a corner in the basement. It came up to my shoulders, and it was awkward for me to hold, too big an instrument for a girl of five. I kept knocking into it as I carried it across the floor, kept tripping over the black rubber cup. But then it occurred to me to turn it upside down and I carried it back upstairs that way — my two hands wrapped around its yellow neck, the black rubber high over my head, facing up, like an enormous flower I had just plucked from some strange, nightmare garden, like a peace offering.

They were still arguing when I got back upstairs, but when they saw me in the doorway there was silence, the violence shaken out of all of their bodies, replaced by sudden calm, a dazed stillness that held the room in place. The scene reminded me of the water-filled dome that sat on my brother's bookshelf: inside, the Capitol building overturned then righted, the snow spinning and whirling and then settling, each reckless flake disappearing, now part of a soft, white blanket, leaving no trace of its singular self, no hint of its wild path downward.

In the shock of this abrupt quiet, everyone felt a bit of shame. I could tell that in addition to the plunger, the very thing they needed, I had brought them this as well. Something like realization passed across their faces. "Oh," my father said. "Oh, isn't that just . . ." His cheeks loosened up, his shoulders looked like mounds of quickly melting snow. My mother hugged me and said, "Thank you," the two words stretched long, rolled out like a rug that conceals stains in the floor underneath. My brother chewed on his fingernails and didn't say anything. His dark eyes darted around the room; I thought of two flies trapped between panes of glass.

It was hard to come to the rescue like this; it was a huge burden for a small girl. And sometimes — not often enough, but sometimes — I rebelled against the responsibility, deliberately choosing the wrong path, the path that no one expected, because it was freedom, release. It was like a girl sinking down into a hot bath, her skin turning pink, her body growing lighter, relaxing.

The next evening, after my bath, which I took in that same bath-room, I refused to get into my pajamas. My mother held the pajama top above me, her fingers pulling the neck open, ready to guide my head through, but I would not give it to her. Instead, I folded myself over in two.

"Okay," she said. "Then let's try with the bottoms." She picked them up and I started to run. She grabbed me at the door, but I squirmed away from her, went down the hall, into my room, into the far corner of my closet. And when she finally caught me, I stomped and screamed.

This was not what I was accustomed to doing, but something drew me to behave this way. There was a release that came from it, from bouncing around inside the snaking alley between pleasure and terror, the place where excitement lived. It felt clean and simple, to know that my behavior was wrong, so clearly wrong; it was a relief to identify with the bad guys. I was not pulled this way and that, but certain, for once, of what I was doing. And somehow I knew, too, that this is what all children did sometimes — they misbehaved, it was their right. I was merely taking what was mine.

For this fit of flailing limbs and shrieking and tears, my mother pun-ished me, sitting on the edge of my bed, bending me over her lap and slapping me on my bare bottom, making it sting, sending shivers down my legs. Each time she raised her arm to strike again, my body held the memory of her hand. I did not try to wriggle free. I had done what I needed to do, there was no point in fighting anymore, this was exactly what I deserved.

She dressed me in my pajamas, and my body was limp, my arms and legs offering no resistance. The top slid right on, warm flannel that made little blue sparks on the way down. When she crouched down to help me with the bottoms, I leaned my head heavily on her shoulder, as though its weight were suddenly just too great for me to manage all on my own.

"I have no idea what got into her," my mother told my father when he came home from work soon afterward, tipping her head in my direc-tion. The three of us were in the kitchen. She was stirring spaghetti in a pot on the stove; I was perched on the stool at the counter.

My father picked me up. "What happened to you today?" he asked. He had the stale, smoky smell of office air. It was not really a question. He kissed me on the cheek and lowered me back onto the stool.

They sat down to dinner in the breakfast room, and my mother decided that I had calmed down enough to join them. I plunked down on the floor in the back corner, behind my father. As my parents talked, I traced the tiles beneath me with my index finger. The fake brick was laid out in a parquet pattern, each piece joined by fake cement, and I followed line after bumpy gray line, zigzagging back and forth across my little section of the floor, concentrating hard, like I was working my way through a maze. My bottom still tingled a bit, like soda bubbles popping at the back of my throat, just enough to make me aware of the surface of my skin. I leaned into the two walls behind me; it was a pleasant, reassuring pressure.

How good it felt to be punished every once in a while, to be reminded that I was a little girl who needed assistance, who would falter unless she was given clear guidance. It was the sweetest, most exquisite kind of pain, like losing a tooth, which left a raw spot that tasted of blood, a tender, aching hole my tongue could not stop returning to.

What a relief it was to be put in my place, the slap from my mother or father reiterating the outline of my being, underscoring the exact dimensions of my freedom. *You will go this far*, the stinging flesh told me, the red ghost of a hand on my skin. *You will go this far and no farther.* There wasn't much leeway, really; there were, blessedly, many ways to go wrong.

On the floor there, I was no higher than my parents' knees. Their conversation ran like a sheltering canopy over my head. It was too far up to reach, not worth listening to anyway: it was grown-up talk, it was beyond me.

My Brother's Room

During the school year, my brother's room always looked "like a tornado hit it," as I often heard my mother saying, with varying levels of anxiety in her voice. No one was allowed entry without his permission, which there was no chance he would grant her, so she could never get in to straighten up. He had certain safeguards in place to ensure that she was obeying this rule. For example, he might put a crease in his sheet before leaving for school, and if it was changed in any way when he got home, he would know what she'd been up to. Sometimes he brushed up the pile of the carpet around the threshold, so that it was impossible to step in without leaving a telltale impression. On other occasions he pulled a hair out of his head and closed it into his bedroom door on his way out.

It's not that he worried my mother would actually clean up; he would have noticed that right away, even without the help of his secret booby traps. I could tell by the way he tensed up when she went in there, his every muscle poised as though he were a wild animal protecting its turf, that his concern was much less specific: he was worried about her mere presence in his bedroom, the fact that she might intrude upon his space with her own will and intention, that she might touch the things that were his, rearrange the molecules in the air with each breath, that she might permeate, alter, ruin.

The cleaning lady, who came to our house every Monday and Thursday, was exempted from my brother's regulation: my mother would only let him go so far. But he didn't actually mind her being in there. She often got confused and put my shirts in his drawers, or his underwear in my father's drawers, and there were a lot of Tuesday and Friday mornings when we all spent a few minutes trading laundry. But Danny had no real connection to her; she was just a person trying to do her job. And while it was annoying to reach into his drawer and find the shirt he had outgrown four years ago folded neatly at the top, the mistakes Almeda made did not threaten him in the way that my mother's fingers simply grazing the stamp collecting magazines on his night table surely did.

The deal was, though, that before he left for camp he had to put his things away, and that while he was gone the no-entry rule would be suspended, so Almeda, with my mother providing the reinforcements, could do the heavy-duty work that needed to get done. The door was open all summer long, and since I was home during those months — still too young for sleepaway myself — I often wandered in and snooped around, trying to uncover clues to his identity, trying to discover his secrets.

Once Almeda and my mother had done their work, the room immediately took on an aged and stuffy feel, even though the windows were always open. It was so neat and clean that it seemed more like a shrine to someone really lost — a son who had been killed in a car crash years ago, with everything exactly as it had been the day the news arrived — than the room of a living, breathing boy who would be coming home, suntanned and taller, in eight weeks. They vacuumed and polished the soft, dark smells of growing — oily skin, dirty socks, deep, sound sleep — right out of the room and replaced them with the scent of Lemon Pledge. The room became a place of memory instead of experience.

I lay down on my brother's bed, swung around in his swivel chair, opened his closet door, looked out his windows. I walked slowly around the room, listening to the floor creak under my weight, feeling the pile of the brown and white shag carpet creep up between my toes, each thread as high as a blade of freshly cut grass.

His room was wallpapered in brown plaid, except for one section, which was covered with corkboard; it was a place for him to hang pictures and birthday cards and first-place ribbons. There was always plenty of space, since he never used it much anyway. It was mostly my father who hung things there, prouder of his son than my brother was of himself. There was one thing, though, that Danny tacked up himself and which hung there for a couple of years: a piece of loose-leaf paper, tracking my payments toward the debt I owed him from a bet. We were sitting in his room one Saturday after a family game of

Scrabble (no keeping score since we didn't write on Shabbat), and he asked me whether I thought that from a lying-down position, he could throw one of the letters into the bag, which I happened to be holding in my lap at the other side of the room. I was all for the bet, which seemed like a sure thing: the bag was small and far away from him, the angle was bad, the letter was too light to throw accurately. But just my luck, he popped it right in. The wager was twenty-five million dollars.

Since I had no actual money, we worked out an arrangement whereby I could pay off my debt through various services. A half-hour back rub, for instance, counted for fifty cents, and each chore I did for him was worth twenty-five. Every punch I endured without crying out for my parents brought me ten cents closer to freedom.

A wooden furniture unit, with a desk, two chests of drawers, and a bookcase, ran the length of one wall. It was stained dark except at one side, where he sawed off the end when he was younger, and on the desktop, where he had scratched away at the finish with his compass. My mother gave him a desk blotter after that, but it didn't cover the whole desk, and you could still see the nicks along the outer edges.

His class pictures were propped up on the desk in their cardboard frames, one small individual portrait, with his hair plastered across his forehead in chunks like dark fingers, and a big photograph of the entire class. In pictures, his smile never came from the inside; the expression was forced. He didn't always know how to respond to the cues the world was giving him; he had to fake it sometimes.

The top drawer held his report cards, thin sheets of pink paper marked up with blue carbon. I marveled at them. I had just started to get report cards myself, and the "E" column (for "excellent") was almost solid with checks, with a couple here and there straying over one box to the right. But his had checkmarks all over the grid, and their placement varied wildly, even from quarter to quarter. My teachers didn't write much about me, since there was never anything new to add, no noteworthy developments. His teachers, on the other hand, always seemed to have a lot to say; they had to scrunch up their handwriting to fit their comments into the allotted box. "He has difficulty paying attention in class," one teacher wrote, "and his performance doesn't match his capabilities. If only he applied himself, he could do a better job." And then, "The quality of his work has improved over the course of the quarter; he really seems to be applying himself." And after that, "The quality of his work has deteriorated, which comes as a surprise given his improvements earlier in the year. He needs to work harder at applying himself." I could not believe how interesting he was, how special, to warrant so much talk, to stump them the way he did. I envied his ability to defy expectation.

In the bottom desk drawer was his stamp collection — a thick binder with a soft vinyl cover, along with plastic index card boxes for the stray stamps that couldn't be matched up in the book. It began with a few foreign stamps from our grandfather and quickly became his obsession. My brother normally tore through life on sheer impulse, all limbs and sweat and violent outbursts, but when he worked with his stamps, his whole being came to a halt. He developed an elaborate filing system. He meticulously recorded each new entry, along with its market value and comments about its condition. He held each stamp with tweezers as delicately as if it were a butterfly, examining it, front and back, under a magnifying glass, and then gently sliding it back into its glassine envelope. He knew exactly where everything was at all times.

Naturally, once his collection got off the ground, I had to start one of my own, but I discovered different reasons to keep at it. The absolute concreteness of the stamps attracted me, and the feeling of ownership, of accumulation. And while he was concerned with watermarks and limited issues and damaged corners, I judged the value of a stamp by its beauty. I wanted bright colors and odd shapes, and though I loved the crinkle of glassine envelopes, I preferred to paste my stamps right into the book, knowing full well that I was rendering them unsalable, so I could see them better when I flipped through its pages.

He tried to teach me what it meant to be a real collector, and though I never fully understood the principles, I made an effort to adhere to them, which turned me into an easy target. Tricking me into believing that I was getting a good deal, he would trade worthless stamps out of his collection for the best stamps from mine. Sometimes he would tell me how he had fleeced me the moment our stamps changed hands, insisting that a deal was a deal and I should have done my research. But then, at age eleven, he let me off the hook — at least in this regard — by officially incorporating as the Heads-Up Stamp Company (the first of many entrepreneurial enterprises) and moving to the big time. He ordered subscriptions to the philatelists' magazines, he went to local shows and drove hard bargains with sixty-year-old men, he paid taxes. My junky collection no longer interested him; he had bigger fish to fry.

The bookcase above his desk was filled with books from school — *The Old Man and the Sea*, *Great Tales of Action and Adventure*, *The Last of the Mohicans*. They were in perfect condition, their spines intact, though he had dutifully written his name on the inside cover of each of them. When I was a few years older, I often turned to my parents' shelves if I had finished that week's library book early. There was the bookcase in the basement, filled with musty paperbacks whose pages were always in danger of crumbling in my hands, and the bookcase in the living room, which held hardcovers that my parents had to pull down for me. But I never touched my brother's books. There was too much attached to them: the memory of my mother chasing him through the house, begging him to try to get through just one chapter, the terrible feeling of excellence, of succeeding where he had failed.

There was also a book of the complete works of M. C. Escher, a slim, tall hardcover my parents had given him, hoping that the logic and math and precision in the drawings might spark his interest in art. And there were a few books on chess; these were well worn, the spines cracked, the covers curling at the corners, the pages dog-eared. He would sit for hours in front of the chessboard in the living room, with a book propped open on the table next to him, studying the moves and strategies of the masters. He chewed his nails, his legs bounced so quickly under the table they seemed to vibrate. He played imaginary opponents, since my father, the only one in the family who knew the game, was hardly a challenge anymore. But sometimes, after reviewing the way the pieces moved and reassuring me that this was all you really needed to know, he would lure me into a game. It didn't matter that I was a much less formidable opponent than my father. With me, he enjoyed the victory, no matter how easily it came. He beat me again and again, in ten moves, in five moves, in three.

My mother sometimes took out books about brothers and sisters from the library for me. In these stories, the siblings fought like crazy, but by the end, their love, which was sometimes difficult for them to express, showed through. And in these stories, little girls always missed their older brothers when they went away — no matter how much teasing and tormenting they'd been forced to endure. But our story seemed different to me, lacking in resolution, lacking the hard cover with crinkly library plastic that I could close with a sigh and put on the table. I didn't feel the way those other sisters did; I couldn't find myself in those pages. While I craved my brother's affection, would do almost anything for his approval, I craved those two months he was gone equally.

The house rested when he was away; you could almost hear it breathing, deeply and calmly. There was no slamming of doors, no punching of walls, no loud bangs as things were thrown to the floor. Every creak of wood sounded like a release, the soothing crack of joints that helps you into a deeper stretch. Noises that our daily ruckus normally drowned out now announced themselves amid the silence — the hum of the refrigerator, the buzz of a trapped fly, the toilet flushing on the other side of the house.

Most of all, though, summer smoothed the lines of worry away from my parents' faces, and instead of distributing their attention in small and tightly wrapped segments, they doled it out lazily and without interruption. They didn't have to spend mealtime telling Danny not to jump around the room, not to kick my shins under the table, not to lean back so far in his chair or he'd fall and crack his head open, while I sat silently outside their triangle of rage and hurt, waiting for the dust to settle. Instead, we ate in peace, and I talked as a little girl would, at great length about small things, and they listened. Evenings were no longer stolen by questions and concerns: would he finally take a bath, or stop watching TV and do his homework, or settle down for bed at a decent hour? They took their own leisurely and whimsical course, with one activity running seamlessly into the next.

Postcards would occasionally come from my brother, a couple of sentences at most. "Dear Mom and Dad" — I was never included in the salutation — "Camp is great. We won the track meet." He loved to race around the parched Berkshire fields all day, playing hard and tough with other boys, getting dirty, exhausting himself. He was glad to get away, but I couldn't even stand day camp. I resented being led from dodgeball to soccer in double file, clutching a strange girl's sticky hand, when I could have been at my mother's side, listening to the tick of the grandfather clock as she read the newspaper. The ear infections that hounded me during those summers were my salvation. Pain and fever seemed like a small price to pay for the gift of a whole day in my mother's care, the promise of silverware clinking on the sick tray as she carried it up the stairs to my room.

When he went to college and I had become a problem child in my own right, I wished my brother had never gone away. I longed for the time when he was my parents' focus, the project they held at the heart of their difficult lives, the task they put muscle into, while I was a good girl, a given, someone to be relied on rather than sweated over. But in those days I basked greedily in their attention, by temporary default, like the moon when the sun goes down, and summer was always the shortest season.

Where My Heart Lies

"Hey," Danny whispered to me, leaning across the backseat of the Hertz rental car. "Did you know you look almost exactly like Dumbo?" He started to chant, still keeping his voice low enough that our parents couldn't make out what he was saying up front. "My sister looks like Dumbo, my sister looks like Dumbo."

We were heading back to the motel in Anaheim after our first day at Disneyland. It was a dream come true for an eight-year-old girl, and I was trying not to let his teasing disrupt my good mood.

"Do not do not do not," I whispered back, as much to drown out the sound of his voice as to contest the claim.

My father was wearing a hat with Mickey Mouse ears. I had won it for being the two-hundredth visitor to the Swiss Family Robinson Island that day, but size large was all they had left, so I couldn't wear it. It was a little small on my father; the beanie rested on top of his hair, like the yarmulkes they hand out at a bar mitzvah. When he turned his head quickly, the ears went lopsided, and I had to keep reaching over the headrest to straighten them out for him. The slightest breeze would have blown the hat away, but we had the windows rolled up.

I could tell by the way my father was driving, his shoulders hunched and his head pushed down into his neck, that his back was bothering him. That's what he always said about his back — "It's bothering me" — as though it were some other person, a fifth member of our family, instead of being a part of his own body. And sometimes it felt that way, like something separate and unpredictable and often badly behaved. Later that night he would stand in the middle of the motel room in his Jockey undershirt and briefs, bent forward, letting the top half of his body hang completely limp like he was doing a dead man's float, his head cocked toward the television so he could catch the evening news, upside down.

My mother was turned sideways in her seat, toward him; her knees banged into the gear box whenever we went over a bump. She was pushing back her cuticles with her thumbnail. After she finished with one nail, she straightened her arm out and splayed her fingers like a cat to check her work. Then she went on to the next nail.

Danny quieted down for a minute and started twisting the skin at my elbow. He had been at it like this all day long, pulling my shorts down to my ankles in front of Mickey Mouse, giving me flat tires, calling me baby for any reason he could think of: because I didn't want to drink a milk shake, because I wanted to drink a milk shake, because I changed my mind about the milk shake. He chipped away at me in little pieces, wearing me down, relentless. Every overture he made was a trap — his hand reached out to mine with the promise of a truce and then pulled away at the last minute: *burnt!*

"They don't allow Dumbo look-alikes into Disneyland," he said to me now. "You'll have to wait in the car when we go back tomorrow."

"I do not look like Dumbo," I insisted. "Besides, then why'd they let me in today?"

"Ah-ha! So you *do* look like Dumbo!" He pinched and twisted again.

"So, kids?" My mother turned to us and clapped her hands together. "What was your favorite ride today, huh?" She was trying to derail him.

"The haunted house," I started. "And the pirate's cove." Danny echoed each word in a singsong falsetto, wrinkling his nose and wagging his head side to side.

I felt like I was in that dream I kept having where the monster was coming and I tried to run but my legs wouldn't move fast enough, there was nothing I could do to stop his approach. My voice melted into a long, slow wail. The tears were a simple reaction, more an acknowledgment of my own powerlessness than a complaint. But the crying jolted my father like an alarm. His face brightened and his fingers gripped the steering wheel tighter.

It was always this way when the four of us were together, and though we were in California on our winter vacation, things were no different here. Danny acted up, didn't listen, put up a fight with my parents about everything: taking a bath, putting on a jacket because it was cold outside, being nice for once to his little sister, not running off on his own and scaring them both half to death. My mother kept saying she just wanted to relax, this was a vacation after all, but every day got loud with arguments, doors slamming, my brother's protests sounding crackly and shrill. He was twelve and his voice was losing its balance.

"Daniel," my father said, looking at my brother through the rearview mirror, his forehead wrinkly, squeezed together. "This is the last time I'm going to tell you to stop teasing her."

My mother started tapping the window with her fingernail, frantically, like a woodpecker. "Oh, Debbie, look!" She was pointing to the flowers planted on the meridian. "Do you see the size of those tulips? Aren't they beautiful?"

Danny smiled at the back of my father's head, his mouth half open, a complex grid of silver wire. "Like I care?" he said, putting extra emphasis into each word. It sounded wrong, like someone wearing headphones and singing along, loudly and off-key. His eyes were wild. He thought this was play, the same as a game of chess where he wowed my father with a strategic move.

"Well, don't you think —" my mother started, but then she realized he wasn't talking to her. She uttered a tiny "Oh"; it was like the click of a door locking. She turned back to me. "Hmm, Deb? What do you think?"

I couldn't focus, couldn't respond. I wanted to peel back those last few minutes and start again. Sometimes I could figure out exactly what to do: I could find the plunger in the basement, I could make the bad things good again, I could get us all back on track. But sometimes, before I even knew it, I was making the bad things happen.

If only I hadn't cried out, I thought. If I had thought to sock my brother in the arm instead. Then *I* would have gotten in trouble, and that would have been the end of it. Now I could see where this was headed, it was getting hotter in the car, the space was getting smaller, something terrible would happen. We were going and going and I couldn't undo any of it.

There were moments when it felt like we were living in a house of cards, everything in such precarious balance, one false move and we all came tumbling down.

Suddenly, Danny reached over and pushed the Mickey Mouse hat forward on my father's head. The back edge of the brim caught on the top of his sunglasses. His whole face was covered.

We swerved hard to the left. The car screeched like the cars on detective shows; I had never heard that kind of noise in real life. My father shook the ears off his face and into my mother's lap and wrenched us back over to the right just in time to avoid sideswiping a pickup truck in the next lane. "Damnit, Danny!" he screamed. His eyes were bulging, and there was a thin film of sweat on his skin. His whole face glowed.

My mother's left knee slammed into the gear box. "Oww," she said, rubbing it with the palm of her hand and then sucking in hard. "Oww." No one paid any attention.

We pulled into a Chevron station, Danny and I flying up out of our seats as we vaulted over the dip on the way in. My father put the car into park between the two islands, blocking off the gas pumps from entering cars. "Damnit!" he said again, slamming his fist down on the steering wheel.

Danny was all defense now, afraid. I could see his Adam's apple slide up and down when he swallowed. Everything had gone sour. My father unbuckled his seat belt and wrenched the top half of his body around toward the back, but before he could do or say anything, Danny said, "Fuck you!"

It was like popping a balloon, it came out suddenly and startled everyone, even Danny. We all flinched at the sound of his words. They hung in the air like the ghost from a camera flash. I blinked the last tears out of my eyes, waiting to see what would happen next.

My father pointed to the road, a busy downtown four-laner. "Get out of the car!" The end of his index finger touched the window and left a smudge when he pulled it away.

"Fine!" said Danny. He punched the lock down with his fist before slamming the door shut.

My mother let out a squeak. Her eyes glistened, her nose started to run; she was trying not to cry, but the tears found a way of seeping out. She groped around in her pocketbook for a tissue, opened it up like a prayer book and then blew hard. I got up on my knees and looked out the back as we pulled away. My brother looked so small inside the frame of the window, alone on the sidewalk, with cars zooming by at his side. He was walking slowly in the direction of our car, bouncing off the balls of his feet with each step, getting smaller every second. His hands were shoved into his pockets and his lips were puckered like he was whistling, no big deal, but I knew he couldn't really whistle and the only sound that came through his teeth when he tried was a thin hiss. It was late afternoon, there was a wind blowing through the tops of the palm trees, and I wondered if he would get cold out there. I was always the one who ended up safe and protected, adored. He was always skittering around on the outside, frantic and alone.

Then we made a right turn and I lost him.

I flipped around in my seat, panicked. "What if he can't find his way?" I asked the back of my father's head. "What if it gets dark out?" I looked up at the sky. "What if it starts to rain? Are we far from the motel?" My mother looked at him like she was waiting for answers, too. She tooted again into the tissue, without taking her eyes off of him. The ball at the end of her nose was bright red.

"He'll be fine," my father said to me, his voice a little shaky. "I promise." My mother kept looking at him, searching his face for something else, a different response, her dark eyes darting around crazily, like water bugs.

"He'll be fine," he said again. He was staring straight ahead, his jaws working. My mother put her head against the window and closed her eyes.

They were separate now, curled up into their own private spaces. I moved over to the exact middle of the backseat, my back perfectly straight, my hands at my sides. The interior of the car was slate gray, the fabric on the seat shiny if I brushed it one way, dull if I brushed it the other way. I swept the fingers of my left hand toward the back of the car. Shiny. I did the same on the right side, to make it match. Sweep, sweep, left. Sweep, sweep, right. And then I reversed the movement. Sweep, left. Dull. Sweep, right. Dull.

Was I even on the inside, too? Was my body like those paintings we used to make in first grade, where you smeared a piece of paper with paint any old way and then folded it, pressing hard, so that when you opened it back up each splotch had a mirror image? If I folded myself in half, would everything match?

Sometimes I had to go inside myself; I had to find a reliable place, a place where there was symmetry.

"Mom," I asked, "where is your heart?"

"Hmm?" She was looking out the window now and stroking the Mickey Mouse hat like it was a kitten. I waited for her to turn around.

"Where is your heart?" I repeated. "In your body." I pointed to the center of my chest.

"The left side, right here," she said, laying her hand flat across her breast. Her face clouded over. "No, wait a minute. Is it the right?" She shook her head vigorously a few times, like she was clearing an Etch-a-Sketch screen. "Goodness, Debbie, I can't remember. You'll have to ask Dad."

I looked at the back of my father's head, scrunched down into his shoulders, and then closed my eyes. Sweep, left. Sweep, right. I could make it even.

Emergency 51

For my brother and me, play was physical, brutal, nearly wordless. It involved pushing, twisting, wrestling, the commandeering of flesh. Our mouths made stupid sounds: grunts and gasps and shrieks; occasionally, squealing laughter. We played together over the course of what seemed like hours piled upon hours, on weekends, when our parents were napping, the world still and flat, the tiny space we occupied charged: he and I barely tolerated each other's presence, but on those long dull afternoons we drew closer anyway. I found him, he found me, both of us pulled toward the simple distraction of company, the thrill of aching rage.

There was a game that he and I were especially fond of. We could do it anywhere, under any circumstances. Our play never started out this way, but this is where we almost always wound up.

He would be chasing me around the yard, or wrestling me in his room, or swinging me in circles by my ankles in the basement, when suddenly —

He pushed me hard into the prickly bushes and little beads of blood rose up to the surface of the skin all along my arms; he let a punch fly in the middle of our wrestling match and knocked the wind right out of me; he dropped me, head first, onto the concrete floor of the basement.

Whatever it was, he had done some kind of damage; he had, once again, gone too far.

I would start to cry. It was the kind of crying fit where my face immediately brightened and crinkled with the wave of pain washing through me, but there was a lag of several seconds before any sound emerged. We waited frozen, hanging, for the noise to catch up to the drama — as though we were both looking at me from far away. It seemed there were hours in which to consider what kind of trouble Danny might get into, how he had messed up this time, the exact dimensions of his failure. It was a moment that was both satisfying and frightening: I was furious at him and wanted him to get punished; at the same time, I didn't want our parents ever to know.

Once the wailing began, Danny backed up and ran, and for a moment I thought he was simply leaving me there, crumpled up on the floor in the corner, or rolling around on the ground outside, and the fury bubbled up in me all over again. But he always returned, blaring like an ambulance siren, circling and swooping at dramatic angles in a jog that was graceful but edgy, a little too contained, as though what he really wanted to do was just bolt.

He cupped his hands over his mouth. "Emergency 51!" he yelled, trying to make his voice crackle as though it were coming off a radio wire. "Emergency 51!" It was the name of our favorite TV show, an hour-long drama about a team of paramedics whose skills each week were put to the test as they were confronted with another medical crisis.

"Emergency 51!" This was the call to action that came to the firehouse from the dispatcher. When the guys on the team, who were sitting around playing cards and eating their brown bag lunches, heard it on the radio, they dropped everything, sprang forward, rushed to save people's lives. The ambulance sailed gleaming out of the garage, the red lights twinkled and swirled, almost festive, the men on the crew were no longer average guys but heroes in the making.

Danny did the siren blare a few more times and then dropped down by my side.

"Vital stats!" he ordered, his eyebrows pulled together as though this were all very serious business. Then he obeyed himself. He grabbed my wrist and pretended to check my pulse, he peeled apart the lids of one eye and waved an imaginary flashlight in front of my pupil. He checked for broken bones by lifting up an arm or a leg and wiggling it, then plunking it back down. At the end of the examination, he rattled off a combination of important-sounding letters and numbers.

By then I was at full attention, wiping away the last of my tears, giggling at my brother's antics, waiting to see what he would do next.

"Patient is smiling," he said to himself. "Nice work."

In part Emergency 51 was an act of self-preservation. If Danny could distract me sufficiently from whatever pain he had inflicted, our parents wouldn't find out, and then he wouldn't get into trouble.

But there was something else that pulled him, pulled both of us, into this game.

Danny was considered a problem child. He could not sit still at mealtime, he fought every instruction, he had trouble making meaning out of black letters on a white page. He was a boy our parents wrung their hands over and argued about well into the night. I, on the other hand, was well behaved, I did what was expected of me. Where I was concerned, everything fell into place according to plan. I was already reading well past my age level; sound and shape meshed easily for me, like the teeth of a zipper interlocking. It was just one more way in which I had overshadowed him.

When we played together, Danny did not realize the strength of his own limbs, or recognize the force with which he wanted to do damage, knocking me back down to the size of little sister, like a cartoon character that can be beaten and banged into any shape the assailant cares to imagine. Before he knew what was happening, he had hurt me. There was the potential for discipline; there was evidence that he really deserved it. We were scared.

Through Emergency 5 1, order returned to us. I submitted willingly to his poking and prodding, which was not really all that gentle; I reveled in his goofy imitation of the paramedics, sleeves rolled up, focused on the task at hand. He was my older brother; I gladly restored him to supremacy by lying there as he undid the damage, softened the bruises, erased the scratches, rescued me, his head looming over me like the sun.

There was a grandness with which Danny played the part, an eagerness with which he launched into the role. In those moments he rose in his own mind, became something, I could practically see it, like a hood peeling back to reveal broad, open features. He was a hero like the men on TV. He knew exactly what he was doing, there were no missteps, there was nothing to regret. My brother — the problem child, the difficult, struggling boy — became all-powerful. He could injure and heal, he could reverse things in an instant, like a strong tide spilling itself upward against the shore and then slinking back, retreating to expose a beach as smooth as glass, not a grain of sand out of place. My brother had stabilized the patient: me, a little girl, her arms and legs intact, her lungs taking in and expelling air at an appropriate rate, her pulse returned to normal, a quiet thump, like the gentle, butting gesture a cat makes again and again against its master's forehead, polite and insistent, full of gratitude.

Sanctuary

I.

We were sitting around the breakfast room table, playing Monopoly. As usual, Danny owned all the real estate and had a huge pile of cash by his elbow. My mother and I had teamed up since I still didn't exactly understand how to play, and we were losing big; my father was in a respectable second place.

I hated Monopoly and would rather have been playing Boggle, but it was Friday night, Shabbat had started, and we couldn't use a pen to write down words. We weren't supposed to handle money, either, and even talk of business transactions was taboo; but my father said Monopoly money was okay, and if we discussed the sale of Park Place or Boardwalk, it wasn't so bad.

The meat tablecloth was still on the table from dinner. It had the same check pattern as the dairy tablecloth, except with brown squares instead of blue. This made sense to me: brown was the color of meat, blue was the color of skim milk, which is what we drank. The fabric was a crinkly plastic that cleaned with the swipe of a sponge. My skin stuck to it if I stayed in the same position for too long, and twice already I had shaken all the pieces on the board out of place by lifting my arm up too suddenly.

Our turn. My mother and I were sent straight to jail.

My mother had been getting up between turns to dry dishes. Now she went into the kitchen to take care of the few that were left. On the way back in, she paused in the doorway for a split second, and then turned off the light in the kitchen with her elbow.

But it was Shabbat, and on Shabbat you did not tamper with electricity. You left on whatever lights you were going to need from sundown on Friday until Saturday night. You left the light in the bedroom turned off for all of Shabbat, and you stumbled around a bit in the dark as you got into bed; you made do.

My father glared at my mother but didn't say anything. My brother and I jumped on her.

"Mom, you can't do that!" We were beside ourselves with outrage. Danny and I both attended Jewish day schools, where we spent half the day studying Hebrew, reading sacred texts, learning all the minutiae of Jewish law. We liked knowing the rules, being versed in this immense body of knowledge. They were fun for us, they gave us a sense of accomplishment; it was almost like learning how to play a complicated game. And it was a thrill to know it was so easy to go wrong and offend God, to get ourselves to stay just this side of divine punishment. We liked giving ourselves a good scare; we ended up feeling safer.

We also liked ganging up on my mother. We didn't pretend not to take sides. Whenever my parents argued, Danny and I adopted my father's stance, parroted his words. We both gravitated toward him, used him as a touchstone. I hate to say it, but we respected him more. There was such satisfaction in uniting against her.

My mother stood there now; she shrugged her shoulders in response.

She couldn't bear to see the electricity going when it didn't need to be, all those pennies you might as well have been throwing right into the trash. She was always reminding us that my father didn't own ConEd, and if we left our TV show in the den for a minute or two to get a snack in the kitchen, we'd better have turned off the light before heading down the hall, otherwise we'd hear about it. But this wasn't a good enough reason now, on Friday night. She needed some other justification.

"Well, Rabbi Goldberg says you can turn lights off as long as you use your elbow." She pointed to her own elbow for clarification. Danny and I looked at our father to see how he was reacting. He dipped his head a little to the side, squinted and furrowed his brow — a *what-kind-of-nonsense-is-this?* face.

We turned back to our mother.

"And especially during the energy crisis," she added, her bottom lip pushed out slightly.

II.

It was a windy Saturday morning, and my mother and I were in the kitchen making tuna salad for lunch. She cut up the celery and red onion into little squares, and I stirred them into the bowl with a warped wooden spoon. A long, low branch of the maple tree kept brushing up against the side of the house like a dog scratching an itch. "We'll have to get that pruned in the spring," she said, looking out the window above the sink. Tiny dots of snow whirled around outside. She shuddered.

On a day like that, hot soup would have been much better than cold tuna fish, but we did not cook on Shabbat. Even though the pilot light was always on, keeping warm a section of the stove top just big enough to fit my hands, turning on the burners counted as making a fire, so we could not use the stove.

My father and Danny were at *shul*, and I usually went with them, but this morning I decided to stay home. My mother never seemed to want to go anymore, and I didn't want to leave her behind. Today she said it was too bitter cold, and she just didn't feel like catching pneumonia on the walk over. She made my father and Danny tie their scarves tight around their necks before leaving.

Except for the wind and the knocking of the maple, the house was quiet, perfectly calm. I was still in my pajamas, my mother was in her robe, and I could hear the shuffle of her slippers as she walked around the kitchen, could hear the sound of my own breath.

A little before one o'clock, my father and Danny came up the driveway, their footsteps sounding like echoes of each other, and then *whoosh*, the front door opening and the cold air coming inside with them. They moved around the house, upstairs, downstairs, changing clothes, washing up, leafing through the mail, which they could not open because on Shabbat you're not supposed to tear. My mother followed after them, dish towel in hand, and asked questions. *So what's going on in the outside world? Who did you sit next to today? What did the rabbi talk about?*

My father said, "You should have come today if you want to know so badly." The whole house was awake and stirring now and the world flowed into it. I could not shut it out, standing there in the kitchen, warming my hands on the stove.

III.

From age eleven through about age fourteen, Danny went through a devout phase.

First, he decided he had to use tissues instead of toilet paper on Shabbat, because when you pull the paper off the roll to wipe you are actually tearing.

"But it's perforated!" my mother cried, at the end of her rope.

"Doesn't matter," he said, carrying his box of Kleenex into the bathroom and shutting the door behind him.

Next, he said he wouldn't blow his nose because the tissue might rip.

"Then use a handkerchief, at least," said my mother.

"Gross!" said my brother. He sniffed back hard instead.

At summer camp he drove the staff crazy; it was a Jewish camp that served kosher food, but he was always in the kitchen around mealtime, making sure they prepared things according to the laws of *kashrut*. At home, he led us in the after-meal prayer, chanting so quickly no one could keep up, as though speed was somehow correlated with piety. On Shabbat, he avoided contact with items that suggest forbidden activities. If my mother asked him to clear the table for dinner Friday night, he wouldn't pick up the newspaper if there was a pencil resting on top of it from when she had been doing the crossword puzzle earlier in the day. He wouldn't put on a pair of pants if there was money in the pockets. "*Muktzah!*" he yelled, dropping them to the floor in horror as soon as he heard the coins jangle. The word refers to items that shouldn't be touched, or even in view, because they might tempt you to violate the rules of Shabbat.

He took it much further than any of us; even my father told him to mellow out.

The rest of the world was a mystery, full of systems and conventions he could not comprehend. He looked at the clutter of black marks on the page in front of him; they swam and danced, they resisted arranging themselves into meaning. He didn't realize when he had pushed my father to the limit — couldn't pick up on his tensed jaw, the change in his voice — and suddenly there was yelling, and punishment. He laughed at a girl with crooked teeth — really, he thought she looked so funny — and the rest of us clucked our tongues in disapproval. Life could be bewildering, so difficult to predict and negotiate.

But when it came to the laws of Jewish observance, Danny was a master. He clung to the rules; they anchored him, made him powerful. It reassured him to be able to rule out certain behaviors and activities, to be able to say yes, this, but not that, to have answers.

Through these years, Danny hardly ever went to *shul*. He found nothing in the prayers, in the gathering of voices. His was a solitary, self-imposed stringency, a discipline enacted for a private end.

IV.

Technically, Shabbat doesn't end until about an hour after the sun sets on Saturday, when three stars have emerged in the purple sky. My mother always cheated it. She took a peek at the sky through the kitchen window and a peek at the clock and said, "Okay, kids, it's dark enough." She started the dishwasher like she had been itching to run it for the last twenty-four hours, and then went all over the house turning off lights.

But my brother and I ran out into the yard and stood there, our heads tilted back, pointing upward, until we found three stars that we could agree on. (On cloudy nights, we were forced to consult the United Jewish Appeal calendar, which generally sets the end of Shabbat at an hour and thirteen minutes after sundown.) This process could take a while, since I was apparently not very good at identifying stars, and the ones I thought I saw sometimes turned out to be planes, or flecks of sky dust, or for some other reason Danny couldn't quite explain didn't meet with his approval. But eventually we saw them, steady, irrefutable lights in the sky. And then, for us, Shabbat was over. Danny went right to the TV, hoping to catch the last half hour of "Dukes of Hazzard"; I headed upstairs and started my homework.

My father was the only one who didn't seem eager to make the transition. When we came inside to give him the okay, he didn't spring forward into action like the rest of us did. Sometimes he'd pick up a felt-tip pen and do the Sunday *Times* crossword puzzle, which came with the Saturday paper. He'd already worked out most of the answers in his head over the course of the day, so it was mainly just a matter of filling in the blanks. He'd straighten up his desk, or start to review a contract or a brief, or call his mother in Florida — but these were all small gestures, and he made them slowly. Even on Sunday morning, he still absentmindedly hummed the tunes from *shul* the day before. The memory of Shabbat lingered; he was in no hurry to say good-bye.

Sometimes he gathered us around the breakfast room table to say *havdallah*, the ceremony that signals the transition from Shabbat to the rest of the week, though for him it was really a way to hold on longer. He lit a braided candle, the weave of separate strands obscured by wax that had dripped down the sides on previous Saturday nights and then dried there, like a frozen waterfall. He said a prayer and then passed the spice box around. We inhaled the clove scent. We held our hands up to the candle and looked at the reflection of the light in our fingernails. In the background, we heard the dishwasher change cycles.

In all the prayers we said, Shabbat has a regal, feminine presence; she is referred to as a queen who graced our home with her weekly visits. It is the woman's role to announce this guest's arrival by lighting candles on Friday evening, the man's to announce her departure on Saturday. But it seemed that in our family, the roles should have been reversed, with my father welcoming the Shabbat queen once again with a big smile and open arms, my mother grabbing her by the elbow and ushering her hurriedly out the door.

V.

When my mother lit the candles on Friday night, she used a paper napkin to cover her head. Her short hair shot straight up for an inch or so before curving off to the right, making a kind of ledge; the napkin sat on top, an almost see-through white square imprinted with paisleys. My father said this was disrespectful, he wished she would use a proper head covering, a real scarf, instead of a plain old napkin, the same kind we used at the table every day.

She wrinkled her nose at the mention of a proper head covering. She thought that a real scarf would make her look too much like the Orthodox women we saw when we went to the Lower East Side to shop for bargains. They were all thick-bodied, frumpy, no flesh showing except on their faces and hands. They wore dark stockings, terrible shoes, and scarves in garish patterns to cover their heads. They had warts.

So she used the napkin, which showed God some respect but didn't turn her into a frumpy *rebbetzen*, rabbi's wife. Nor did it jeopardize the lift in her hair.

The candles sat on the sideboard in the dining room, in front of the old-fashioned, convex mirror that hung on the wall. I stood in the doorway and watched my mother in the mirror, which spread her face wide and turned her shoulders into withered little bumps. She went through the blessing, her head tipped down slightly, her hands covering her eyes. Then she moved on to her own private prayers. This part could be long or short, depending on how well or badly behaved Danny had been lately, and whether anyone in our family was sick. She spoke so quickly and softly it was impossible to decipher her words. If I asked her what she was saying, she wouldn't tell me. "I was talking to God," she said, "not you."

My mother broke rules, cut corners, bridled at the restrictions an observant life imposed — and yet for all that, she seemed to have a more personal connection to God than my father did. When she prayed, it was with passion. She whispered her special requests and promises and believed there was a powerful presence somewhere out there in the universe that heard her, considered her words, responded appropriately. When she prayed, she actually talked to God.

The God that my father prayed to was inherited, ancient and abstract; there was no intimate, one-on-one dialogue. For him, prayer and observance were a way to be closer to his own people, their collective past, to feel more strongly the tethers and the embrace of community. He made the decision when he was in college to have this kind of household, to raise his children in this way; the home he himself grew up in was culturally Jewish but not observant. He had reconnected; he had reinforced a weakened link.

My mother told him that religion was a private thing. "It's something personal," she said, "something everyone needs to figure out for themselves."

"That's what religion *means*," my father said, his shoulders drawing together with anger, "when we all agree on the rules as a community, when we do what our ancestors did. Otherwise everyone's just doing their own thing and what does it even mean to be a Jew anymore?"

The rules, he said, were not for us to make up as we went along; they were for us to carry out. What she was talking about — he threw his hands up in the air, a dismissal — was a free-for-all.

At *shul* my father shook the hands of the older men, stooped, graying, and in their faces he saw his own ancestors. When he sang the prayers in his booming voice, he heard himself joining in a chorus of millions over time. In Danny and me, he saw another generation carrying tradition forward. This is why his eyes teared up at Danny's bar mitzvah, why he smiled so broadly when Danny and I chattered away in Hebrew at the dinner table, even though he knew the reason we had switched over from English was that we didn't want him or our mother to understand what we were saying. We were the children of Abraham and Sara; we were the future of the Jewish people.

On Shabbat my father did not move into an exalted, spiritual realm; he rooted himself more firmly to the world.

VI.

My father wore his yarmulke around the house on Shabbat, but he always took it off before going outside — even if he was on his way to *shul*. My mother didn't let him out otherwise. Sometimes he tried to sneak through the door, but she always caught him.

"Ed, are you forgetting something?" she would say, and then whisk the yarmulke off of his head. He reached up to his head to grab it, the way you would quickly grab your hat when you felt a gust of wind blowing over you, but he was too late. "Here," my mother said. "You can put it on when you get there."

Sometimes they argued about it. "I'm not forgetting anything," my father told her. "I want to wear it."

"Ed," she said. Her head flopped to the side; her lips pulled back into her cheeks. "Would you please just put the yarmulke away for now?"

"What do you want to hide?" he asked her, cords pushing up inside the skin of his neck. He knew that she responded this way because she had left Austria with her parents in 1939, as a two-year-old with a terrible cough that made the authorities almost deny them exit, and because so many of her relatives hadn't made it out and were killed in the

Holocaust. She spent her childhood trying to fit in and become a good American, mortified by her parents' heavy accent, their poor command of English. He saw her fear, but he saw that there was shame, too, in her reaction.

"Look, Ed, the whole world doesn't have to know you're Jewish. You're an American, too. You should look like one. This is New Rochelle, not some Eastern European *shtetl*."

"And because this is America, I can do this," he told her.

But she always won. My father folded his yarmulke up carefully, like he was wrapping up a diamond, and then tucked it into his suit pocket. He smoothed his hair down. Then he left.

Whenever they had this argument, I sided with my father, but mainly because his position was the one that seemed more noble to me, and because I was in the habit of allying myself with him no matter what. But deep inside, I was rooting for my mother, hoping that once again he would obey her wishes, which were really mine as well. It was a tiny, delicate impulse that expanded and grew more insistent as I got older. When he wore a yarmulke in the street, he looked not like my very own father but like a stranger. He lost all specificity and became a type: the frail, provincial, even backward Jew, trapped in his unenlightened, insular world.

I was always glad when the yarmulke disappeared.

VII.

By the time I was fifteen, all of us except my father had abandoned the trip to *shul*, but for a long while, he didn't stop trying to round up company. At the breakfast table he asked Danny and me: "You kids want to join me today?" He was already dressed in a suit, he had already eaten. He looked like he did during the week — clean and professional and not a hair out of place — except for the stubble on his chin, a sprinkling of red and brown and gray: no shaving on Shabbat.

"Nah," we told him. "Not today." I explained that I had too much reading to do for school. Danny yawned extravagantly and said that after breakfast, he would probably just head back to bed. Then my father asked my mother, who was drinking coffee and reading the newspaper, pulling her robe tighter around her neck no matter what the weather. "Harriet," he said, "how 'bout you?"

"Look, Ed," she told him, defensive and angry. "I just can't. I've got too much to do around the house," though she never said exactly what it was that needed to get done.

"This should be a family thing," my father sometimes said, more to the wall than to any one of us, a private yearning that had somehow made it past his lips. "I want this to be a family thing." He clenched his fist and jerked it inward: it was the same gesture he made when a basketball player on the team he was rooting for missed a shot.

When he spoke that way, I pictured us like the families in the textbooks we had used in grade school: typical, mother-father-sister-brother, sometimes all holding hands. What he wanted was unrealistic, a flattened-out version of our true selves, all our separate and warring impulses dulled, our heads smoothed into perfect circles and our outstretched hands nothing more than clunky mitts — when actually religion was one of the things that split us apart; or perhaps it merely exposed the divisions and petty alliances that already existed.

Still, he did cut a lonely figure, walking down the driveway, turning right down the hill, his dress shoes making a thin scraping sound that hung in the morning air.

VIII.

For me, *shul*, in the beginning, was this: a bright blue carpet, rows and rows of men in suits, here and there a woman in a fancy dress and pumps and a felt hat with a broad brim, maybe a feather sticking out the side; the walls decorated in panels of colored stone, each depicting symbols of one of the Jewish holidays: a menorah and a Maccabean shield for Hannukah, a challah, a cup of wine, and two lit candles for Shabbat. The panel at the end of the row where we always sat had an apple and a pot of honey for Rosh Hashanah. I sometimes walked up to it during the service, traced the hard, round skin of the apple with my fingertips. The cantor sang in a high voice filled with curly flourishes like smoke on its way toward the sky, bouncing on the tips of his toes and grabbing the sides of the lectern with his hands, as though the notes were carrying him up, too, and he had to find a way to keep himself grounded.

The prayers quickly became familiar to me. The Hebrew words were shapes I recognized, though I didn't always know what they meant. I sang along, not needing to understand; the singing had its own pleasures. I tried to carry the tune alongside my father's loud and off-key voice, but I was pulled in the direction of his wayward notes. So I sang quietly.

Sometimes I found my friend Abby and we joined the other kids outside the sanctuary, running up and down the halls, playing hide-and-seek. If we made too much noise, an old man with yellow fingernails came out to quiet us, his *tallis* draped across his shoulders, his index finger pressed against his lips, his face screwed up in anger at our bad manners.

But mostly, s*hul* was time for my father and me. My mother and brother stopped going long before I did, and so for many years it was just the two of us. When the rabbi began his talk, he and I whispered to each other about everything — what the woman in the third row was wearing, why it was that my mother had decided once again not to join us, what the sound of the rabbi's crackly voice reminded us of. From these hushed conversations I memorized the shape of my father's left ear, the smell of his collar, a combination of musk and dry cleaning.

As I got older, *shul* became something else — a routine I had exhausted, a routine that bored me. I no longer felt the dreamy mystery of the place. It seemed like a roadblock, an obstacle, something that was keeping me a child. Week after week I sat through the same three-hour service, while I was growing and changing, new thoughts creeping into consciousness, wishes I had never experienced before. There were other things I would have rather been doing; the kids I knew were never there.

Of course, when I talk about *shul* I am really talking about my father, the way his own wishes constrained me, the way he wanted to stop time. There he was, every Saturday morning, waiting for me at the bottom of the stairs, looking forward to these few hours we would spend together with the same level of enthusiasm, of joy. I saw how much he needed it: a morning one-on-one with his little girl.

The girl who was also, in a way, a surrogate wife. Over the years, our conversations during the rabbi's talk took on a different character, became unpleasant. He would tell me that I was so sensitive, so perceptive, that our tastes and values were the same, that I knew how to wear clothing, unlike my mother, that I looked fabulous in my Shabbat dress.

His eyebrows began to bother me; they were so unruly, curling this way and that, extending from his forehead like wings. More and more, I noticed the odor of his breath. When he spoke to me, I could no longer lean in close.

But still, for a while, I listened. Danny so easily made excuses on Saturday mornings, or managed to sleep until noon. I was more dutiful; I had to learn to let my father down. I had to force myself to say no. It took years. He was such a kind, intelligent man, and my mother was so out of touch with what he needed, that it really pleased me, on one level, to satisfy his longing for companionship. I felt alive, my whole being infused with purpose, as we sat side by side in that enormous room, with its high ceiling, its stained-glass windows, sun from the skylight above the dais warming our heads, pouring in on us like wisdom, like a blessing from something divine.

The Rules of the Game

The Mets were playing the Cardinals at Shea Stadium, and we were there, the four of us, seated in the usual fashion: parent, child, parent, child. Danny and I were separated by my father, who was the most in demand; my mother was on the other side of me.

Though my father and brother had been going to baseball games together for years, this was my first, and I felt particularly grown up that day, one of the boys. My mother receded in this context; her denim culottes and espadrilles were dark shapes along the edge of what I saw.

I was wearing my navy blue windbreaker, a hand-me-down from my brother, one of my favorite pieces of clothing. On the back of the jacket, in a slight curve of white capital letters, it said *Winadu*, the name of the sleepaway camp Danny had been going to for the last few summers. Danny had outgrown the jacket a couple of years earlier, and I was finally big enough to wear it, though I still had to fold back the cuffs a couple of times.

My father was swiveling back and forth between my brother and me, quickly switching roles as he turned. With my brother, he played a fan caught up in the excitement. *What a hit! Oh, jeez, did you see that catch? Did that look like a strike to you, Dan?* With me, he stepped outside the action and became a teacher explaining the rules, his index finger pointing to the little men below. He leaned as close to me as possible so we had the same perspective on the baseball diamond, but with his head right next to mine, it felt like he was letting me in on a secret. *Do you see, Debbie, why he's walking? Watch the guy on first closely now; he's going to try to steal second.* An error. A foul. The end of an inning. It all looked so strange and formal to me, like a dance, the field as neat and stylized as a stage set, players and umpires in their costumes, their bodies engaged in prescribed movements: rule-bound, systematic. It was a kind of choreography.

Whenever my father leaned over and explained something to me, my mother asked him to repeat himself so she could hear, too. She had been to only a couple of baseball games herself.

"Why did you say the guy walked?" she asked him. "How come he didn't run to third? Come on, Ed, speak up."

My father seemed suddenly weary. He had no patience for her questions.

"As I just explained, Harriet — " he began.

"Look, I don't always remember it the first time, okay?"

"But if you would just *listen* to me, Harriet, and think about what I'm telling you — okay? — then you might."

In theory my father was a Mets fan; he was a loyal man with a strong homing instinct, someone who thought that roots were everything, that history defined you, and to turn your back on where you came from was the worst kind of betrayal. The friends he had were the ones he had made in junior high school and at sleepaway camp. The house we lived in was just two blocks from the house he had grown up in, and though my grandparents didn't live there anymore, moving there from our apartment in Riverdale was still a return to the idea of home, the notion of family, and, in any case, familiar ground. He could watch his own kids running up and down the streets he had played on; he could listen to the memory of his mother calling after him that dinner was ready, come on in and wash up.

He complained about how quickly loyalties shifted these days. "When I was a kid," he said, "if you lived in New York you rooted for the Brooklyn Dodgers, period. No matter how badly they were doing. These days everyone just wants to be with the winner."

But my father's loyalty competed with another impulse, which was to root for the underdog, who he believed needed his support more, and whom he couldn't help feeling bad for. He was plagued by guilt when his team won. Best-case scenario for my father: the New York team was losing, which is exactly what was happening now.

The people all around us were rambunctious; they seemed close to exploding, and the atmosphere felt restless, a little bit crackly, as though it were filled with the static you hear just before a record comes on. They seemed to have come in packs of ten and twenty: whole rows of men who knew each other, slapped each other on the back, yelled teasing remarks that I didn't understand from one end to the other. They laughed hard. It was difficult to tell who they were rooting for, their whoops of delight sounded so much like their cries of dismay. They were drinking beer, eating hot dogs, throwing all kinds of trash on the ground. It was a windy day: crumpled-up napkins danced down the steps and then spun up into the air; paper bags skittered across the aisles, flung themselves against the backs of people's seats, then slid down and flew off.

My father and I both caught sight of a plastic cup rolling back and forth in the aisle on our left.

"At Yankee Stadium," he told me, "the fans are much better behaved. This is the worst kind of crowd you'll ever see." A strip of thinning hair blew into his eyes as he talked; he smoothed it back in place. The wind immediately whipped it forward again.

A few minutes later, a plastic drink lid fell from the sky and landed on the front of my jacket, right where Danny's name would have been if my mother had paid to have it personalized. It stuck there. When I peeled it off, it left a yellow crescent of mustard against the navy nylon fabric.

Before I had time to react, my father smoothed the strip of hair into place again, this time with force, and charged out into the aisle and then up a few steps to the nearest landing. He was positioned like an actor on his little rectangle of cement stage, projecting his voice, a dramatic monologue for this section of the crowd. He seemed at once small and enormous.

"If so much as a single piece of trash blows down here," he bellowed to everyone behind us, the ten rows of spectators, leaning so far in their direction I thought he might fall over, jabbing at the air with his index finger, "I'm telling you right now, you're going to be damned sorry!" His face was red, his eyes were bulging, I had no idea what would happen next. "Damned sorry!" he repeated.

There was a pocket of quiet for a moment or two, a tiny, sudden stillness in this one section of the stadium — it felt as if even the wind had stopped — and then my father sat back down.

My mother pulled a tissue from her pocketbook and wiped most of the mustard off my jacket. "There," she said, loudly enough for my father to hear. "We'll get the rest off at home." Then she turned to him.

"Goodness, Ed! No wonder your blood pressure is so high. You're going to give yourself a heart attack one of these days." Whenever he got worked up she became the calm one, acting as though she'd never gotten upset in her life.

My father didn't say anything, just stared at her, blinking hard, his jaw working with the stubborn rhythm of a pulse.

It was unsettling to have him so close to me right now. Instead of feeling safe, I felt prickly, on edge. His body seemed too alive with energy. In the moment of rushing to protect me, he had become a force I suddenly could not count on, as prone to whimsy as the pigeons on the field below, gathering themselves messily into a nervous gray cloud for no apparent reason, all dirty wings and sharp beaks, and flying away.

There was a naive kind of romance in what my father had done, a chivalry that didn't really apply: in this stadium filled with men, he was playing the part of the savior, as though he were the prince rescuing the princess from the dragon, as though there were no other way to express his love than by defending me.

And as I traced the phantom crescent of mustard on my chest, the shadow of my mother suddenly asserted itself; her presence took on flesh and weight. I knew that she was part of the reason my father behaved this way — all of his masculine love funneled toward me, squeezed tight when it should have been diffused, becoming its own strong and unwieldy force, bursting forth into this single inconsequential moment. I understood that his loyalty was also an act of infidelity, that there is always a side that loses.

And I saw how it was possible to love someone too much, how devotion could turn jagged and unbecoming, leading to threats and bravado, twisting everything out of proportion, breaking the rules of the game, bases loaded, batter up, an umpire in the distance crying, *Play ball, play ball.*

Ring Fingers

ost of the married women I saw — my aunts, my mother's friends, my teachers — wore both rings on the same finger, the one I learned to call the ring finger. The wedding ring was closer to the rest of the body, and, one of these women told me long ago, therefore closer to the heart. This order made sense to me: the marriage representing a deepening of affection, an amplification of sentiment and regard. Sometimes the rings matched so well it was hard to tell, when I looked at these women's fingers, where one ended and the other began. The two together looked like one big ring, engagement leading seamlessly into marriage.

But my mother didn't wear both rings on the same finger. She wore her engagement ring on her right hand, her wedding ring on her left. She explained to me that she did this because the rings were too big to fit on one finger. The engagement ring was *S*-shaped, like a sea horse, full of diamonds, the head and tail stretching out past the circle of the ring itself, almost from knuckle to knuckle. The wedding ring took up a lot of space, too: four separate bands of gold that climbed up her finger.

"You know, I didn't think I could wear this engagement ring when I first saw it," she told me one day. It was summertime, Danny was at sleepaway camp, and we were planting pansies in the urns that sat at the front door of our house. My mother had noticed the dark soil collecting around the diamonds, packing itself in, and had stopped what she was doing to scrape it away with her fingernail. It was pansies every year, though my father always wanted her to try another kind of flower for a change.

"How about something different this year, Har?" he would say. And she would tell him to stop criticizing, or she would say, "I'll think about it," or she would just leave the room as though he hadn't said a word at all.

There was something about my mother's tone now that made me feel like I was finally old enough to hear a secret, and I sat still, waiting for her to continue.

"It seemed so fancy," she said, "so different from what other people wore. But Dad wanted to get me something that was one-of-a-kind, something special. He didn't want me walking around looking like every other engaged woman in 1960." It was strange for me to hear the ring ever felt foreign, because it seemed to be a part of her now: I expected the flash of glitter when her hand moved across my field of vision, the cluster of raised, hard rocks when I grabbed onto her fingers.

As I got older, the unhappiness of my parents' marriage came into better focus; it was no longer a painful part of the landscape of our home but something that stuck out, a problem worth considering. My parents were not only my mother and father but two people with too much silence between them. I saw the daily disappointments, the way each of them was proven, again and again, not to be the person the other had wished for. Their pairing became a puzzle.

Perhaps this is what growing up was about for me — not a mastery of new skills, a stepping into life, but an increasing discomfort with what had formerly been a given — an unsettling. Perhaps it was the unraveling of a story I had always lived with, the neat plot slowly losing its momentum, collapsing, and then, after that, it was the challenge of opening myself up to make room for a more complicated story, bumpier, less polished. Perhaps that is the story I am trying to tell you now.

I could not say simply, "I don't understand," and be done with it. It was nearly intolerable for me to witness the way they were together, engaged in the same conflicts night after night. It was grueling and also boring in the most exhausting way: my mother serving the same bland meal, the plain spaghetti sticking together, curled up in hanks inside the bowl, the broccoli once again overcooked to almost mush, army green, my father coming home after a long day at work, snorting and rolling his eyes as she brought the food to the table; or my father telling my mother how to walk down the winding staircase, the way his own mother did, turned a little to the side, ankle crossing ankle, one hand barely touching the banister as though it were the skin of a new lover, instead of letting her descend her own way: faced forward, inelegant, *clump, clump*.

As a teenager, I sometimes climbed the stairs to our musty attic on weekend mornings to poke around in the boxes of memorabilia that were stacked there. I didn't go up there with a conscious agenda, but somewhere I knew that what I was trying to do by sorting through these scraps of history was find evidence that would help solve the mystery of what drew this poorly matched couple together, because maybe understanding would make life easier for me: a nostril close up is a hideous thing, but when you see it in the context of a face it's not so bad.

I had to resort to this kind of sleuthing because when I asked my parents directly how they ended up with each other, neither of them told me much, though they made it clear that hope had a lot to do with it.

"I thought she'd be a good wife, a good mother," my father said. "She was very beautiful."

"He had his head on straight," my mother said. "He was so self-assured. He knew exactly what he wanted out of life, out of the future."

Sitting on a box in the attic, I sifted through handmade birthday and Valentine's Day cards my father sent my mother during their courtship and engagement, little notes he wrote her in calligraphy for no special occasion, poems filled with corny rhymes and illustrated with rudimentary sketches in the margins. Occasionally, I came across a card from my mother — something store-bought, uninspired.

I was interested in boys in the most basic and abstract way at that point — as a species whose behavior I might someday understand — and had yet had no firsthand experience with passion, but still, I knew that it was missing from this correspondence: there was nothing like a specific and unique connection between two individuals, or the sense of two odd shapes locking in together, fitting, or the reverence for another person's psychic bumps and crevices, a landscape worth tracing a thousand times over.

What I saw was that they were playing roles: my father almost generically romantic, taken with the gestures of love as much as the emotion itself, and my mother self-consciously, purposefully distant, as infatuated with her stance as my father was with his, enjoying the way he wooed and courted her, believing this was her right. It must have been easy for them; before they were married, they spent so little time together.

On one of these trips to the attic, I came across a letter my father wrote my mother before their wedding. In it, there was news of life on the army base, where he was in basic training, and then, at the end, a sketch of a wedding gown with a low back and off-the-shoulder sleeves. There was an arrow pointing to his picture. "By the way," he wrote, "I think your wedding dress should look like this." He had ideas for her.

I knew from their wedding photos that the dress she ended up wearing looked entirely different, a scoop-necked gown with three-quarter sleeves and buttons all the way up the back: already, even at the altar, an expectation she could not meet, a rebellion she felt compelled to enact. It was the first of many challenges.

Over the years, the way my mother wore her rings began to make another kind of sense to me. I started to see the engagement and marriage as discrete and unrelated stages of her life, distinct in feel and tone: of course the rings should be on separate fingers. The engagement ring was magical, tipped at a jaunty angle, full of sparkle. The wedding ring was modest, unadorned, in need of polishing, as though the reality of the marriage itself could never live up to the engagement's dazzling promise.

Triangles

By the time I was nine, there was an atmosphere of conspiracy in the house. My father and I were partners: intertwined, exclusive, my brother off doing his own thing, my mother circling, circling, wanting in.

My father made jokes at the dinner table that my mother didn't get, and then he and I laughed together, because I understood.

"You two," my mother said. "Like peas in a pod." I beamed. It was such an honor.

He and I did the crossword puzzle together, marking over my mother's faintly penciled guesswork with the correct letters, written in black pen in an identical bold hand. We chuckled at her mistakes; we sneered at the lack of rigor in her reasoning. We took walks around the neighborhood after Shabbat dinner when she was too cold to go outside. We talked about ourselves and the world and the qualities we sought most in a brownie (the best was dense and moist but not soft; no nuts) while she wrinkled her nose at the thought of so much sugar and fat.

I gave him what my mother could not.

And he gave me what my mother could not: a certain stability, a sense of security. When I wanted to cry because a horse had been shot on television, he let me. He put his arm around me and he said, "Yes, it is sad, isn't it?" I felt safe when I was around him; he was solid and constant.

On Saturday afternoons, when my brother was working on his stamp collection, or playing chess, or sleeping, the door to his room shut, and my mother was in the kitchen, putting away knives or wiping streaks out of the glassware, he and I sometimes looked through art books together. He was a lawyer who loved his job, but he always said that in another life he would have been a painter. When the four of us went for drives in the country, he took one hand off the steering wheel and made quick marks in the air, holding an imaginary pencil between his thumb and forefinger, doing phantom sketches of the trees as we flew past them. In his study there were stacks of sketch pads and art supplies that he almost never touched: delicate brushes, little jars of ink, pencils with shiny gray tips. And in the living room was a small collection of art books.

On the bottom shelf of the bookcase, there were several slim books that were part of a series —*Art through the Ages*— though for some reason, we didn't have the entire collection. My father and I skipped past the books that dealt with the art of the Far East and ancient Greece and the Middle Ages. Neither of us had any interest in these, and their covers were in almost perfect condition, their spines intact. Instead, we went back again and again to the books with the paintings where there were figures in action, their muscles twisted like ropes, their limbs flung out in all directions, the paintings where there were stories being told: the art of the high Renaissance and beyond — up until the late nineteenth century, when it got harder once again to imagine yourself walking into the painted world, when space was no longer realistic.

I grabbed one of these books from the shelf, and my father and I sat down close together on the rust-colored velvet sofa. He held the book in his lap and I leaned up against him. I got to turn the pages.

These were old and well-worn books. The covers were soft along the edges from repeated handling, and the spines were so broken in that the books held themselves open, even when we were close to the beginning or the end. The tissue paper that covered each color plate was yellowed and dried out like molted snake skin, with little cracks working their way in from the sides; it was almost impossible to turn the pages without ripping them a little more. And even though I'd never seen the originals, I could tell that the colors were off, just like the color photographs that filled up the beginning pages of our photo albums: the blues were too green, the reds were a bit muddied, the flesh tones were gray, as though the atmosphere in these paintings were contaminated with a fine spray of ash.

Unfortunately, many of the paintings in these books had a religious theme, and we were required to breeze quickly past them: Christ doing this or that, annunciations, assumptions, an endless assortment of saints, the Madonna and child painted a hundred different ways. Old Testament scenes were acceptable, though, as were depictions of events from Greek mythology. Sometimes we were tricked by painters like Caravaggio and Velázquez, who made New Testament characters look like everyday people, and it was not until we looked at the caption that we realized we had been studying the calling of St. Matthew or the supper at Emmaus.

We lingered over the paintings by Titian and Raphael and Rubens, where there was a tumble of naked or barely clothed bodies, limbs swirling and arcing, fabric loose and flowing, everything leading you in circles around the page. My father followed these circles lightly with his index finger: in Raphael's *Galatea*, the arch of a cherub's back at the bottom of the painting drawing your eye up the outstretched leg of a satyr on the right, which pulls you up to the top of the canvas, where three cherubs poised with bow and arrow form a dome over the scene and move you back down on the left.

"Do you see this?" he asked me. "Do you see how this moves?"

But the paintings that really amazed him were the ones with the triangles. They made him suck in his breath and then let it out in a big, appreciative sigh. They made him smile, though his joy was circumscribed, edged with the faintest sadness, the longing to produce such beauty himself.

"Oh, look at this one," he said to me, his voice quiet with awe, when we turned to Gericault's *Raft of the Medusa*. "Do you see how it's all really made up of triangles?"

I shook my head no. The painting looked like pure chaos to me: a fragile craft tossed about by rough waters and crowded with people, some scrambling to right themselves, full of panic, others exhausted or dying, their bodies slack.

"Try squinting," he said. "It's easier to see the triangles that way." And then he started to show them to me. First, the biggest triangle of all. The base points were created by two prone figures at the back of the raft; a crowd of figures reaching forward, piling up on the canvas, formed the triangle's two sides, which funneled into the third point, the peak: a single figure, waving a torn piece of clothing wildly into the distance, seeking rescue from a faraway ship.

Once my father pointed out this triangle, it wasn't hard to find others. The canvas was filled with triangles, large and small; they were everywhere. I saw that the painting was carefully arranged, the disparate parts organized around a single shape, duplicated all over the canvas. There was order beneath the crisis.

Was it from these Saturday afternoon lessons that I learned that the whole world could be studied and read, that if you paid attention to the details of a moment, you would find that they added up to something bigger, more important?

"Do you see how these triangles create stability?" my father said. "That's why we enjoy looking at these paintings so much. There is something about a triangle . . ."

To him, this was the most pleasing art: when there was an underlying balance, when the scene could be reduced to a fixed, reassuring shape. The specifics of Gericault's painting dissolved in front of our squinting eyes, replaced by a basic form — solid, enduring, incapable of collapse.

When my father and I had been in the living room for a while, my mother started finding reasons to come in and check on us. First she decided she had to water the plants that sat beneath the window. Then she came back with a rag to wipe the dust off the mantel and the picture frames on the wall. Then she went up and down the stairs a few times, poking her head through the door on the way.

Every time she checked on us, I could feel a shift in energy in the room. My father looked up from the page and tracked her movements. Sometimes he'd stop talking midsentence. It was as if the whole room were holding its breath until she left.

Finally she came in and said, "So what are you guys up to, quiet as mice in here? Can I join you?"

My father chuckled quietly, though when I looked at his face it seemed he was closer to crying. Then he made room for her on the couch. We turned some more pages, but something had changed. My father and I didn't talk as freely with my mother there; we didn't pause at each color plate. I knew that when we finished with this book, we wouldn't get started on another one. Neither of us really wanted her there; she was an interference.

"Wait; back up, back up," said my mother.

"We've already gone through those, Harriet," said my father — impatient, annoyed.

"Yeah, Mom, we've already gone through them." I was exasperated too.

"Okay, okay," said my mother. "Back off, you guys."

We turned our attention to the book in my father's lap again.

"Oh, Ed, remember when we saw that one at the Louvre."

"It wasn't the Louvre, it was the Prado."

"No, no. It was the Louvre. I remember Fran and Joel were with us. It was summertime. It was the Louvre."

"It was the Prado, Harriet." My father's voice was rising. "Look, it says so right here." He was mad not about this simple mistake but about all the times she insisted on her point of view despite the evidence. I understood that, but still I felt bad for her, suddenly, for the way he and I were always so quick to exclude her.

"Okay," I told my father. "So she made a mistake."

"Yeah, Ed," she said. She took her cues from me, sticking up for herself if I'd already spoken in her defense, otherwise letting it go. I could step out of place and just like that, the balance would shift; I had that much power, that much responsibility.

Her back straightened, her chest puffed up. "Big deal. I made a mistake."

"I'm sorry," he said quietly, looking more at me than at her. "You're right."

We turned some more pages.

"Hey, that looks like a Rembrandt," I said when we came to a yellow-brown portrait with dramatic light.

"That's incredible," my father said. "Kiddo, you're just terrific."

"Amazing, Deb," said my mother. "You really have an eye."

She smiled at my father; he turned his head and smiled at me. Even his pride was something he could not share with her.

I looked away, off into the distance, waving my torn piece of cloth, scanning for a ship on the horizon.

Story Time

Perhaps, by now, you have a clear picture of the people in my family; perhaps you even feel as if you sort of know them. And yet you can't help noticing that I, the main character, come across more muted, a little fuzzy. It is harder to get a sense of who I was. Maybe that deficit makes for a less satisfying read. If so, I apologize. But how could I tend to my own experience? How could I know what was going on inside? I had other, more important things to do.

There were so many bad feelings in that house: the current of rage running between my parents, their wit's-end frustration with Danny, Danny's own anger and frustration at a world he had such trouble negotiating, my mother's distractedness, her day-to-day sadness, disappointments all around.

These things flew, hovered, landed like birds. They were not like the baby robin that fell from the sky and then took off again, full of promise, healed. They were menacing, and they stuck around, like the crows I used to see near the train station when my mother and I went to pick up my father at the end of the day, their shrieks cutting the air, their dark feathers gleaming. They were so huge they seemed stuffed, unreal.

Where I looked there were dark beasts with beady eyes, there was the milky splatter of fresh shit. But I never heard anyone talking about any of this.

Here is what I heard instead: Danny and I were given the best education, and quality time with our parents, and enriching experiences. We were taken on trips to nature centers and museums; we visited our grandparents in California and Florida; we were not latchkey kids. Our parents were not getting divorced like the parents of some of our classmates; those people shirked responsibility, they were selfish, undisciplined. Our home was safe and nurturing; you could walk in at any time of day and it would be spotless, no dishes piled high in the sink, a sure sign of neglect.

So we were a happy family, a good family, a family with excellent values.

Still, I saw those things in the air, I felt them, I absorbed them. And in a way, that gave me some power, a kind of mastery: I could catalogue the subtleties of what I saw, I could be in charge. I could be the keeper of all that was unacknowledged; I could arrange everything however I wanted. I took note of my father's clenched jaw, and the fear escaping from my brother's lips. I registered every one of my mother's soft sighs. These things became my own.

But there was no room inside of me to hold all of what I saw and pay attention to my own experience at the same time. I pushed those emotions to the side; they got flattened, buried. I made that sacrifice. It was safer, in a way: what devastating rage and terrible disappointment would I have discovered had I granted my feelings permission to rise?

I must have felt the absence on some level. I must have been searching in my own quiet way. I must have known there was a self that needed tending to, that was being collapsed, crowded out: a self that was in danger. I think I did what I could, little pulses and pushes to rescue myself, find myself, prevent myself from dying.

I became desperately curious about my own history, as though looking to see where I had gone to, to find the girl I believed I must have been, bring her back to life. It was a kind of detective work.

"What was I like as a baby?" I would ask my mother. "As a very little girl? What do you remember?" I became insistent, full of dire need: I wanted stories, more stories, again and again.

Who could I turn to for help with this project but my mother? She had created me; she had been there all along; she was a grown-up. But perhaps there was something more that pushed me to push her, something telling me that she decided who I was, that I could not know myself except through her. The picture she painted was off, out of proportion, the colors all wrong, but it was the only one I ever recognized.

Here is one story she told me: When I was born, my mother was so exhausted, so doped up, hanging by such a thin thread to consciousness, that she did not hear my father correctly when he leaned over, kissed her sweaty cheek, and whispered, "It's a girl."

"Another boy?" she asked him, yawning. "Oh, fine." And then she fell into a deep and restful sleep. She and my father actually wanted a girl, but she was not disappointed by what she thought she heard in the split second before she passed out. Mostly, she was relieved that the ordeal was over.

My mother always exaggerated the "out of it" part. "I was so out of it I couldn't even see straight," she told me one time. Another time: "I was so out of it I barely knew who Daddy was."

Both my parents found this anecdote amusing: to think that my mother could have gotten *that* wrong. And besides, they reminded me with every telling, the story had such a happy ending! My mother was doubly delighted when she finally came to: not only was I a healthy baby, but I was also a healthy baby *girl*! I was invited to imagine what a pleasant surprise I was, to consider how much joy I gave my mother simply by being exactly who I was.

But I did not find the story entertaining or reassuring. I could not take it at face value; it pointed to something, it disturbed me. I focused on the initial mistake, rather than the resolution. I pictured my mother in her hospital bed, her thick, dark hair pushed up in a wedge against the pillow, her eyelids beginning to flutter. She pulled off from the dock of awareness and into her dreams with the wrong information stowed away in her groggy head, the details of my being unattended. I felt like I was glimpsing the beginning.

In the very first moments of my life, and at the most basic level, my mother mistook me for something I was not. The very first words she uttered about me — a self-assured pronouncement that conflicted with fact. Bright red and puffy, my lungs still clearing out, I was already misread. Already, there was the assumption that I was one thing, when in essence I was actually another.

There were other stories, too. Sometimes, on Sunday mornings, the four of us sat in my parents' bed, and my mother would tell us what she remembered about Danny and me.

When she told stories about my brother, scenes I had not witnessed or had no way of remembering came to life. For example: The four of us were riding an elevator. I was two, in a stroller; Danny was six. A friendly and unsuspecting stranger, trying to engage Danny in conversation, asked if I was his baby sister.

"No," he said, poker-faced. "She's my baby uncle."

My mother remembered one terrible night when Danny decided he didn't want noodles and cottage cheese for dinner. In protest, he threw his entire meal against the living room wall, one tiny fistful at a time. Seated in his high chair, the food compressing into a paste in his hand, then launching, he was red first with rage, and then glee.

She talked about how in fourth grade he came home from school tipsy, weaving as he made his way up the driveway: he had guzzled Kedem wine at a Purim party; it was so sweet he had assumed it was grape juice.

She said that when he was a toddler and they were still living in the city, he would scramble along the sidewalk looking for cigarette butts and then try to eat them.

Danny was such an animated character in these stories, so full of attitude and fiery will. The stories my mother told about me were sweet, perhaps, but very boring. The contrast always saddened me.

She said that as a baby, I hardly ever cried. When I first learned speech, I said adorable, intelligent things. On a plane ride to Florida to visit my father's parents, delighted with my newly discovered ability to communicate, I toddled up and down the aisles introducing myself to the other passengers and collecting their salt and pepper packets. At three, I offered my grandmother coffee when she came over for a visit, having recognized that this was her preferred beverage.

"Gamma want coffee?" is what I am reported to have said.

Even as a child, I found these stories dull; I recognized that some essential spark of life was missing from them. I asked my mother if she could remember anything else, anything more interesting. I pressed her with a desperate insistence. I wanted her to be able to tell the kind of stories she told about Danny. I was ashamed to see that this was all I was, all I had been.

My mother could never make sense of my disappointment.

"But you were so wonderful," she would insist. "You were delicious. A delight."

I felt trapped when she told me this, so envious of my brother, who had the permission to squeeze his fist hard around trouble, the freedom to reach for bad things.

I started to tell my own stories, too.

"Remember when I almost broke my hand in the car door?" I asked my mother one day. My brother had just broken his arm on the school bus — roughhousing gone too far — and the incident must have jogged my memory.

"That's not exactly what happened," my mother gently corrected. "You came out just fine, none the worse for wear, no damage at all." She kissed my fingertips.

"Perfect," she said.

Here is what happened that day:

I was at my friend Robin Askowitz's house, a Sunday play date. It was the end of the day, the yolk of the sun was bleeding into the sky like a barely cooked egg, and my parents had come to pick me up. Robin's parents invited them inside. "Come on, stay a bit," her mother said. "I'll brew a pot of coffee." There was the scraping of metal across the linoleum floor as they all settled in at the table, then the tumble and spill of grown-up conversation.

Robin and I knew we now had a good half hour left of play, so we snuck out of the kitchen and into the driveway, which was the kind of driveway I loved, smooth black tar, still warm from the day's heat.

Robin wanted to show me a new doll that was in the backseat of her parents' car. I didn't play with dolls much, but she assured me this one was special. It was a Barbie and she had the most beautiful blond hair, and the kit that she came in had a brush and barrettes, as well as several changes of clothing. Robin opened the heavy door of her parents' silver Ford, and I grabbed onto the frame and leaned in to watch her as she dug through baseball gloves, candy wrappers, yellowed newspaper, until she found what she was looking for. Robin swung the Barbie up off the seat by the handle of her case and put her down onto the driveway. Then she slammed the door shut, pushing with all her might, right onto my hand.

A pulse of pain shot from my fingers all the way up my arm, as though I had been squeezing a block of ice. I started shrieking; the sound seemed to come from somewhere outside my own face, a pure and icy noise that touched the sky. Then Robin was screaming, too, her blue eyes were big with tears, her freckles disappearing into the red of her face. Barbie was on the ground, not blinking, staring out at us from inside her pink plastic case.

Everyone rushed out of the house, the car door was opened, I was whisked inside and a big ice pack was placed on my hand. The grown-ups leaned over me, fussing, their breath smelling of coffee.

Robin's father called one of their neighbors, an orthopedic surgeon, who came over to the house to examine my hand. He held it up, pressed gently on the pads of my fingertips, wiggled my fingers, rotated my wrist. No broken bones, no swelling even, just a little soreness. I got a clean bill of health.

The grown-ups were relieved, their tense bodies loosened and spread, Robin's mother poured refills. "Thank god for the slipshod construction of American cars," someone said.

This is not how I remembered the incident. What I remembered — and remember still — is this: I was not at Robin's house but the house of another friend, Orah Edelman. *Orah* means "light" in Hebrew. Her auburn hair, tied up in two tight ponytails, shone in the setting sun.

And as I remembered it, it was the father of the little girl whose name meant light who was the doctor in the story. He was a radiologist, and he took x-rays of my hand. When they were done processing, he slid the thick sheets of film into the light box against the wall. In the darkened room, Orah's father and I looked at the x-rays.

There was my hand, suspended against the light box, the bones coming through a grayish blue, luminous. I was amazed that I looked this way on the inside, an assortment of bamboo sticks that didn't quite connect, each finger broken up into discrete, suspended segments. I wondered how such a fragile collection of pieces could possibly hold me together, could really provide the framework for my body, could help me move and make my way through the world.

And I was shocked that there was nothing special about the hand, nothing I recognized, nothing that said who I was. The fingers didn't look stubby, the meat of the palm was gone, there were no fingernails with chips of pink polish on top and thin rings of dirt underneath. The hand could have been anyone's; it could have belonged to my mother, or to Robin, or to the skeleton in my brother's science class.

I remember pulling out of the driveway in the back of my parents' car later on, the ice around my hand beginning to melt, quick drips splashing onto my thigh. And I remember looking out the back window at the big Tudor with heavy, dark beams on the outside, though really the house at which this all took place was brick. I stared at those beams: a series of them shooting straight up in parallel lines, others branching out of them along the angle of the roofline.

It was as though I could clearly see the way the house stood up, as though what was holding it all together was not a mystery of construction and things about the world that I didn't yet understand but a self-evident, lackluster pronouncement, a simple matter of following the path of one thick, sturdy beam until it met the next and then the next across the flesh-colored exterior of the house.

This is what memory did for me: used fact as raw material, a springboard from which to reach another kind of truth. It took the rough outline of events and transformed what really happened into something else: what should have happened, what would have happened, if all the knobs and scratches on the surface of each day served as perfect symbols, outward signs of the churn and pull deep inside us.

There is more drama in this version of the story, of course, but there is also this: the desire to look past skin, to get to the very center, to find out what was truly mine. There is the wish to recognize something familiar in the bones of my body, an exclusive, telltale mark that designates an immutable identity. There is the need to see the fingers of my own hand, splayed out in a fragile fan of bones, lit from behind: my own self waving back at me.

Shadow Girl

uring the summer after third grade, I finished *Harriet the Spy* in a few sittings. I did most of my reading perched on a branch of the maple tree in my backyard, shaded from the sun by its fingered leaves. By the time I was through, I wanted glasses, and I wanted to be a spy just like Harriet.

This is what always happened when I read a good book: I believed in its reality. I began to think the world in its pages was a world that actually existed, or could at least be constructed without too much difficulty. *The Chronicles of Narnia* convinced me there was a secret passage in my house, too, and for a while I wandered around exploring different closets, coming up against darkness, the swing and weight of heavy coats, the pungent odor of mothballs, searching for an exit. After *A Wrinkle in Time*, all my senses were primed to discover some easily overlooked slit in the surface of everyday experience, a fissure I might slide myself into.

But *Harriet the Spy* seized me like no other book had. Rather than presenting a completely foreign reality that I had to imagine, it offered a more glorious and dramatic version of the one that already existed for me. There was no magic in *Harriet the Spy*: just a girl who noticed things, who sat on staircases listening, hidden from view, who stood in doorways watching, unobserved. A girl like me.

But there was something else; the book was not only inspiring but reassuring. In Harriet's story, the complicated truth about people was always being revealed — that even the most upstanding citizens have their weaknesses, that even the ones you like best have their flaws, even Harriet herself.

In my family things were much simpler. If you were a good girl, like I was, you were all good. My mother called me an angel, my father said I was so kind and thoughtful and selfless he worried that people would take advantage. And yet I knew there were dark things inside of me, pushed so far down I could only sense them: uncomfortable thoughts that were badly pitched, like a narrow staircase in an old abandoned house, monstrous feelings that moved in rumbling clouds.

They had me all wrong. Somehow, inadvertently, I had deceived them. I argued against their descriptions of me; I insisted that they were not the best judges of my character.

But protesting did no good. My parents simply chuckled to themselves; on top of it all, they told me, I was also way too modest. They needed me to be this gift of sugar and spice, the foil to my bad boy brother, who was creeping toward adolescence, yelling and disobeying, neglecting his studies, refusing to sit still.

I didn't try hard enough to convince them; I stopped trying altogether: I needed, too, to give them this gift of myself, to see the delight in their faces as they undid the bow, unwrapped me. They deserved it, after all; they had struggled so much. Besides, there was a nice kind of symmetry this way; there was a balance I was ultimately unwilling to disturb.

I pushed the dark things farther down. It felt like I was living with another girl, a shadowy being who would neither leave me nor make herself known.

Harriet's complex, layered world seemed like a safe place to me; her investigative work was a relief. I liked knowing that there were secrets out there, that everyone had a hidden self.

I tried to convince my mother that my 20/20 vision had suddenly taken a drastic turn for the worse.

"I can't see your face very well," I told her, squinting. "How many fingers are you holding up?"

She looked at me suspiciously.

"We'll get you checked out before school starts," she said. "Like we always do."

Further pleading had no effect.

Undaunted, I armed myself with a pencil and a black-and-white speckled composition book left over from the school year and headed out one Sunday morning to case the two-block area surrounding my house — that was as far away from home as I was allowed to stray. I was determined to uncover something juicy, even without the benefit of little round glasses like Harriet's, which, I reminded myself, had no lenses and were really only for show after all. Who needed them?

I decided to sneak into the Millers' backyard, though in actual fact, there was no sneaking involved: they lived right next door to us, and our yards were separated only by a few sparse bushes. Besides, I often went over there anyway to play with their dachshunds, Sasha and Sam, who spent several hours a day rolling around and humping each other in the outdoor pen that the Millers had built for them.

Today Sasha and Sam were nowhere to be seen, and I was glad. They were sweet but loud-mouthed dogs whose yapping would certainly have blown my cover. I surveyed the setup. The shades were all pulled down in the first-floor windows; no hope on that front. But the garage windows didn't have any curtains, so I focused my efforts there. I carried a patio chair over (simply dragging it across the flagstone terrace would have made too much noise), positioned it just below one of the windows, and climbed up, pencil and notebook in hand. I wiped the dust off the window and tried to take a peek inside. The sun was too bright; all I could see was my own reflection. So I tucked the notebook between my knees, slipped the pencil into the back pocket of my cut-off jeans, and cupped my hands around my face, which was pressed right up against the glass. Now I got a clear view of the whole garage, whose entire contents amounted to one car.

This discovery was a huge disappointment, though I couldn't quite name what I had been hoping to find instead. A dead body would have been nice — I imagined it curled up in one corner under a tarp, toes poking out — but I didn't need anything so dramatic. I would have been happy with a few piles of unidentifiable junk: something that might warrant a closer look, a layer of life poking through, suggesting there was still more to uncover — the way the school librarian's skirt sometimes slid up her legs when she walked down the hall, revealing the slimmest margin of delicate, ivory-colored slip.

But the Millers were a particularly tidy couple; apparently their garage had not been doing double duty as storage space — for dead bodies or anything else. Still, it did boast the singular advantage of having windows, and so, as far as garages went, I didn't have a choice. I checked the time on my digital watch and dutifully made an entry in my notebook: "Sunday, July 15, 10:37 A.M. Miller garage. Contents: one pale yellow Chevy Impala." I thought for a moment and then added: "In good condition."

I moved on, traipsing through perfectly manicured yards and across tar driveways, soft and tacky from the heat, in my blue suede Puma Clydes. I poked my head through the gaps in firm spruce hedges. I looked up at curtained windows and down into parked cars. I listened for strains of conversation — a terrible argument, the plotting of a murder — but all I heard was chirping sparrows and the whoosh of the highway several blocks away. Here and there, I lifted the lid off a trash barrel, prepared to seize some evidence of disarray, only to find a couple of plump garbage bags tied up as neatly as birthday presents, their knots metallic and tight.

I kept wishing I would come across someone unexpectedly and be forced to jump behind a tree or dart around a corner, only narrowly escaping detection, meanwhile catching a glimpse of some private, spontaneous moment. But there was no one around — no bathrobe-clad mothers opening their front doors to snatch the *New York Times* off the top step, the smell of sleep still wrapped around them like a cloud, their faces, without makeup, plain and sagging, flames of hair shooting up from the tops of their heads, the way my own mother looked in the morning. There were no families fighting about who would sit where as they loaded up the car for a day at the beach, the father shouting at the kids, and then at the wife, *Is it even worth it? I mean, what is the point?*, no housekeepers taking out the trash, sneaking a few deep puffs from the half-smoked cigarette they retrieved from their front pocket.

My search came up empty. By the end of the day, I had made just two more entries in my notebook: the Kaufmans' lawn hadn't been mowed in a while, and there was a station wagon that I didn't recognize parked in the Oshlags' driveway. This was not exactly the kind of information to arouse suspicion, especially since I was friends with Diana Kaufman and I knew her family was away for two weeks, and the Oshlags often had weekend visitors. There was nothing going on that would raise any eyebrows. In fact, there was nothing going on at all. My quiet neighborhood just didn't hold a candle to Harriet's bustling Manhattan, where life spilled out of doors and the streets were full of action, where you could leave your Upper East Side apartment building and find yourself smack-dab in the middle of a wild adventure. If there was anything exciting taking place in the New York City suburb of New Rochelle, the drama was unfolding quietly — and behind dead-bolted doors. The whole world seemed sealed shut, polished, perfectly smooth, like the wax fruit my mother kept in a basket on the coffee table: a decorative item that never went bad.

And so, after one uneventful day, I gave up.

I turned the composition book over to my mother, who used the remaining pages as scrap paper for her endless "to-do" lists. But when the fourth grade school year started, I began to write in another notebook. It was a pocket diary with a rinky-dink lock and key that I had to fuss with every time I used it. I had seen it one day at the local variety store and had to have it — not so much because I wanted to write things down, but because I loved the gold-embossed edges and the way that for a few magical seconds the soft burgundy cover held the indentation from my fingertips.

Once I had the diary, though, I used it. I wrote about how much I hated my brother, about how excited I was that my friend Denise would be coming over later that day. But mostly I wrote nasty comments about my classmates and teachers in a nine-year-old girl's exclamatory style: "Josh Rabinowitz always pees in his pants!" "Marty Schwartz smells so bad I feel like throwing up. Plus, he picks his nose in class." "Today, Melanie Jacobs is wearing the ugliest sweater I've ever seen in my whole entire life." "Mr. Friedlander is soooo gross. He cleans his ears with pen caps while we're taking tests and he coughs up his phlegm into paper towels. Disgusting!!!"

It was as though writing down one mean thought unleashed the next, and I was never out of things to say. When I wrote, I bent my head down close to the diary, and the whole world disappeared. There was nothing but the pen and the tiny rectangular page, the thrill of putting down words on paper so thin it was almost see-through. My whole body felt alive, on edge; my heart banged around in my chest, making itself known.

I brought the diary to school with me and recorded my observations, before class started, during recess, whenever I had a free moment. When I was finished writing, I always locked the diary back up. But I did so because it gave me a sense of ownership and I enjoyed jiggling the tiny key, not because I worried that someone might read it. The thought never occurred to me, even though this was exactly the doom that befell Harriet at the end of her story. In fact, I kept the key right there with the diary in my desk.

Perhaps I was so lax about security because I was hoping, somewhere deep down, that my diary would be discovered. Maybe I wanted my teachers and friends and family to find out the truth about me: that I was not the girl they believed I was, that an endless stream of ugly feelings and unkind thoughts flowed through me. I could not tell them this myself. I was afraid to buck their expectations. As things were, they liked me. Would they still?

One day during recess, Marty Schwartz — one of my favorite subjects — snuck into my desk and found the diary. He read it cover to cover, and then promptly turned it over to Mr. Friedlander, who had also received frequent mention in its pages.

The shadow girl had materialized; she was now in full view. But rather than adding shape and weight the way darkness in a painting fills out form, she simply eclipsed the other me. It was somehow impossible to fuse the two. I was a bad person. The words I had written proved it to the world, to me. They erased everything I was before.

Mr. Friedlander clucked and wagged his finger at me.

"You should never say mean things like that," he told me, his eyebrows pulled into the furrows above his nose. "How do you think it makes people feel?" And he began to give me, once his star pupil, the cold-shoulder treatment.

When I got home that afternoon, my mother asked me, in her most casual voice, "Anything interesting happen at school today?"

"Nope," I said, burying my head in the refrigerator to root for a snack. I had a hard time looking her in the eye when I was lying.

"Well, I got a very upsetting phone call from Mr. Friedlander. Do you know what he called about?"

"Um, yeah, I guess so." There was no point in pretending anymore.

"I must say, Debbie, I'm shocked. Absolutely shocked. That you could be so nasty! I just don't know why in the world you would do such a thing!" And I couldn't really tell her why in the world I would do such a thing. I had no reasonable explanation.

My mother never actually punished me for what I had done. She didn't send me to my room, or tell me no TV or talking on the phone for the rest of the week. But I could feel her anger — and worse, her disappointment — in the way she watched me: assessing me, from a distance, looking a little confused, as though a complete stranger had somehow made it into her house undetected.

There was no one to talk to at school the rest of the week. Thanks to Marty Schwartz, the news spread quickly among my classmates, almost none of whom had escaped my private criticism. Even after a round of humiliating public apologies arranged by Mr. Friedlander, I found myself friendless for a few difficult days, which is about as long as kids will hang onto their resentment.

I ate lunch all alone, with the warm, small, slow-motion feeling that always came with great shame. I took the tiniest bites out of my peanut butter and jelly sandwich and chewed each one thoroughly, staring down at my desk the whole time. During recess, I sat by myself in the corner of the playground, bundled up against the cold weather, scratching designs into the pavement with pebbles. In Mr. Friedlander's view, this forced isolation was well deserved and perfectly appropriate: it would give me some time to reflect upon my transgression. And my mother told me that's what you get when you write such terrible things, and maybe I'd think twice the next time I felt the urge to put pen to paper.

I have thought twice, Mom, three times, a hundred. Yet I've done it again: put pen to paper, or, more accurately, fingers to keys, words on a screen. And worse still: I have written something the whole world could pick up and read; there is no lock and key. But I am not pointing fingers now, laying blame, snickering, wrinkling my nose in disgust. I am telling my story: what made me who I am.

My life turned out to be much like Harriet the Spy's after all. Our special notebooks had both been stolen, our innermost thoughts had become public information, and we had been forced to suffer the consequences. But I never made the connection at the time. I had already forgotten about Harriet and did not take comfort in sharing the fate of my one-time heroine, who was now on a bookshelf keeping company with Paddington Bear, the Borrowers, and a slew of other characters who had come into and exited my life.

The diary was eventually returned to me, but I didn't write in it anymore. It sat on my desk for a while before I finally put it away, at the back of my bottom drawer. Sometimes I took it out and touched the soft burgundy cover. Over and over, no matter how hard I pressed, the material caved in beneath my fingers and then puffed up again, like a stubborn heart, intent on beating.

Golden Sparrow

n the middle of fifth grade, I began to fake illness. At least once a week, while the whole class was working quietly on division problems or writing poems about which season was their favorite or, if it was the afternoon, studying Torah or Talmud, I went to the teacher's desk and whispered that I needed to see the nurse, I had a bad headache, or I felt really sick, my stomach was killing me. I rotated teachers and periods so no one would become suspicious, and I was excused every time. I slipped out of the classroom — released — and headed down the brown carpeted hallway to the nurse's office.

On the way, I fine-tuned the details, choosing descriptions that would answer the questions I knew the nurse was going to ask, trying to figure out how to make the symptoms important enough to warrant attention, but not so dire that I lost credibility. *What does the headache feel like?* I imagined myself saying as I put both hands up to my head. *Well, the headache is like a hammer pounding right inside my forehead . . . it's like a line of pain that splits my brain in two . . . it's like a really tight helmet around my skull. The stomachache?* I grimaced here and placed my hands gently across my middle. *I've got that salty sour taste in my throat, that's what always happens before I throw up . . . I've got cramps spreading all over my belly.* By the time I reached the nurse's office, I had almost convinced myself that I was really sick. These were descriptions and gestures I had picked up from my mother. I had heard and seen them so often they felt like my own.

Mrs. Kraus was tall and consistently thick, like a tree trunk; her long face was framed with wiry, sand-colored curls that didn't move. She was not a particularly warm person; she did not put her arm around me or cluck her tongue in sympathy or put her hand on my forehead to gauge my temperature by the more maternal method. She just sat me down on her cot and popped a thermometer in my mouth, strictly business, then turned back to her desk.

On TV I had seen a lot of ESP experts who could bend spoons and make tea cups rise off the table and guess the names of audience members, and I had begun to believe that you could make anything happen if you concentrated. It was almost like wishing — which came naturally enough — but with more discipline and focus. So while the thermometer was in my mouth, the bitter taste of rubbing alcohol spreading across my tongue, I tried to push the mercury up the ladder of degrees by sending it feverish telepathic messages.

It never worked. My temperature was always normal, and Mrs. Kraus delivered the bad news with a few quick shakes of the thermometer and a short sigh, as though she, too, were disappointed. Sometimes she let me rest on her cot anyway until the end of the period, and I spent that time facing into the wall, fingering the minute bumps and blemishes in the plaster, otherwise perfectly still.

I didn't feel unhappy; I was not someone who had difficulty in school, who could not understand her studies, who sat alone at lunch time. I had friends to whisper to in class and play with during recess. There were girls whose houses I visited for sleepovers on weekends. There was a girl who made me laugh so hard during lunch that milk came out my nose. I enjoyed what I was learning; my teachers liked me and were generous with their attention and praise.

Still, lying there on the cot, I was relieved. I felt thankful for the respite, the interruption that put my life on hold for half an hour. Though I was managing it all just fine on the surface, sometimes simply being a kid seemed like too much to me, the spaces through which I moved when I was without my parents filled with too many threats. From them I had learned that the world was a dangerous and inhospitable place. They thought first and always of what might go wrong; they considered everything in terms of its potential risks. Yes, I could go play with Abby, but I should make sure not to ride on the back of her banana seat bike or wear her clogs — I could fall, I could twist an ankle, I could get hurt. No, I couldn't ever go back to Judy's house — not after they picked me up from a play date there once and I had a big dark stain on my jeans from slipping in a grease puddle in her garage. When I was set loose to play with neighborhood kids after school in the warm weather months, the screen door swinging and then banging shut as I took off down the driveway, they didn't yell after me to have fun; instead, they reminded me to be careful.

There was a part of me that remained that playful girl with the grease puddle stain, but her impulses were overlaid with worry: my parents were so fearful for my safety that I learned not to think of myself as anything other than vulnerable, exposed, fragile, not quite capable of handling the task of being a nine-year-old. Rising from sleep so early in the morning into the darkness and cold, a long yellow bus honking and then dragging me away — it felt somehow inappropriate, indecent, a shock to all my senses. Two kids jumped up and down in the aisle all the way to school, trying to figure out why they kept landing in the same spot; the bus launched me into the air with each bump in the road, I felt my bones rattling inside of me every time I landed; someone had stepped in dog poop and the whole bus stank. I looked at the graffiti on the back of the seat in front of me: "Todd wuz here," "Math sucks." I made designs in the fog on my window. All I wanted, really, was to be at home with my mother.

It was dark in the nurse's office, quiet except for the shuffling of papers on her desk, the squeak of a file cabinet drawer opening. I could hear a lesson in progress through the open door of a nearby classroom. The chatter was muffled, not at all intelligible. It sounded like it was coming from a dream.

For as long as I can remember, this is what sickness did for me: rescued me, lifting me out of the dangerous tumble of daily life and returning me home, where I was protected, safe. It brought me back to my mother, and my mother back to me.

Most of the time, she was pulled inward, preoccupied — ill herself, distracted by my brother, or buffeted about by a slew of frightening, nameless worries that drew life from her body, so that she bumped around from task to task with a droop in her spirit and a minimum of energy, like a balloon that's lost some of its air. Her attention was conditional: I was the focus when I had done something to make her proud, but otherwise I slid to the periphery of her awareness — when I was faltering, confused, unsure, or merely trying to negotiate the thousand inconsequential struggles that make up a child's day. She shared in my successes but did not sit with me through the less glorious moments, did not offer advice or sympathy or the gentle pressure of an arm around my shoulder. Instead, she pushed me impatiently, anxiously toward resolution, or she simply retreated in a gust of frustration. Either way, she was quick to move on to other things.

"How did your day go?" she would ask me when I came home from school.

"It was okay," I would tell her, a drag in my voice, my chin nearly touching my chest, "but on the bus Aaron was teasing me."

"Why should that make you so sad?" she asked, already a little agitated.

"Because he said I was dumb," I told her.

"But why should that make you sad? I mean, so what? So what if he said you were dumb?"

And then when I didn't snap out of it, she said my skin was too thin, it would get me into trouble one of these days, and she threw her hands up — a gesture of defeat — and started loading the dishwasher.

Often, in my healthy life, I was disturbed by a sense of longing when I was with her, an uncertainty, a vague apprehension that bordered on mistrust. There was a question stirring in the darkest part of my brain, a worry too deep to be teased forth with words: would she give me what I needed?

One afternoon my father was helping me with a math problem, and suddenly it occurred to me, with a flood of shame: Why was it that I had gone to him, and not my mother, with my question? When I wondered about it out loud, he told me my mother was good for some things, he was good for others, that's what was so great about having two parents. But as I considered his explanation, I realized I had a hard time naming the things my mother was helpful for. I could think of only one instance in which I would choose her over him: when I was ill.

When I was ill my mother seemed to understand exactly what I needed; I had wounds she felt comfortable tending. She was an expert. She knew how to soothe an earache; she knew what pill to pull from the medicine cabinet to make a headache better. She could address each specific complaint with a specific treatment: cough medicine, Tylenol, a bath, a cup of tea, a visit to the doctor, a blanket. My discomfort and pain drew her to me.

She came to school to get me in the middle of the day, and when we arrived home she peeled off my clothes, helped me into clean pajamas, tucked me into bed. She pulled down the shades and turned off the lights and crept out of the room on her toes, turning the knob slowly as she closed the door so it generated only the tiniest click. Of course I was not asleep yet, she knew this, but she was so full of gentleness and caring that she could not help making this gesture. For a long time after she shut the door, I could hear her in the kitchen just below me, finding one more reason not to leave the house: a message being left for the pediatrician, the refrigerator door opening and closing, the water in the sink going on and off, dishes being stacked and returned to cabinets. The sounds were another blanket warming me, a reassuring weight.

She wheeled the TV into my room and I was allowed to watch as much as I wanted, even on Shabbat. She pulled up a chair next to my bed and did needlepoint while I rested, her hand floating up toward the ceiling and then diving back down, a chevron pattern in rust and cream and tan slowly filling in. Her straight-from-the-can cooking style, which I normally complained about, following my father's lead, chiming right in, now suited me perfectly. She heated up cans of chicken soup; she made red Jell-O, hot cereal, toast and jam, plain macaroni, bringing everything up to my room on a tray. She poured me big glasses of orange juice, apple juice, ginger ale; she made tea with lemon and honey. When I was sick, I was soothed and satisfied by so little — extremes of temperature, a bit of texture, some sweetness and some salt.

My brother was a shadow then, something at the edge of vision. He was not allowed into my room because of germs; the closest he was permitted to come was the doorway, though he sometimes leaned his whole body in, making sure to keep his toes behind the threshold. Whatever conflict he and my mother might be having took place downstairs, far out of view, and though I could hear the cadence of voices rising in anger, the words themselves were muffled beyond recognition. In any case what they were arguing about receded to the background; my mother had other priorities, a schedule that overrode the timing of his outbursts. Silverware clinked on the tray; it was time for my medicine. There was a protective wall around me. It was almost like being an only child, my mother's single focus.

My mother left the bedroom door open when she and my father went to bed. And in the middle of the night, when I was chilled and achy, I could cry out to her and she would come, a glass of water and two aspirin in her hand, and she would kiss me when I lay back against my pillows, her cool, dry lips lingering on my cheek.

My father was there, too, of course: rubbing my back until I fell asleep at night, calling a couple of times from work to check in on me, taking an earlier train home so he could sit with me while I ate my dinner in bed. But he was gone for long stretches, he was not the one who filled my requests all day, and besides, there was no major shift in the way that he regarded me. He was consistent and therefore an adjunct in this drama, he played a supporting role.

My mother, on the other hand, was transformed by my illness; when I was sick she came into her own. Her blurry, uncertain edges sharpened, her flesh filled out with the complete weight of her awareness. Whatever illness she herself might be battling at the moment suddenly eased up. She assumed a kind of grace. What a pleasure to be able to restore her to such a station, to give her that authority and power, to reject the oatmeal my father prepared — so thick the spoon stuck straight up inside the bowl! — and tell him that my mother had to make my breakfast, that only she could get it just right. I was giving myself a gift, too: the knowledge that I could rely on her, draw strength from her, lean heavily against her hip as she helped me into the bathroom in the fuzzy light of dawn, wincing along with me as my feverish skin touched the cold porcelain seat.

It was no wonder that I wanted so desperately to leave the fifth grade classroom and flee to Mrs. Kraus, each week describing a slightly different symptom, hoping one of these times she would believe me. It was no wonder that I did what I could to get sick, stay sick, perpetuate the illusion of sickness — running around without a jacket when my mother wasn't looking; surreptitiously touching the kids with colds so I could expose myself to their germs; holding the thermometer up to the light bulb in my night table lamp when I knew it would otherwise read normal; giving in to a cough I had the power to suppress, letting the deep, phlegmy rumble roll through me.

It was no wonder that I loved the taste of erythromycin, the feel of the cool, thick liquid sliding down my throat — though I knew it was like loving a traitor, because the very substance that represented the delicious bliss of sickness was also the thing that healed me. It was no wonder that this was how I marked time, in terms of illness. I did not think of the summer when I was four and went to day camp for the first time as the period during which I had a series of ear infections; I think of the period during which I had a series of ear infections as the time that I also happened to be four and going to day camp.

"I wish I could take it from you," my parents always told me when I was sick, stroking my greasy, flattened out hair, looking kindly into my eyes. I didn't tell them that all the pain and discomfort were worth it to me; I didn't tell them that even if they could have taken it from me, I would never have given it up.

In all of this, my mother was my accomplice. Any sign of illness, and she kept me at home: a runny nose or a temperature that was just a couple of tenths of a degree above normal. And I had to be perfectly healthy for a full forty-eight hours before I could go back to school because, she reasoned, my immune system was susceptible and I needed some extra time to build up my strength. She said that going back to school the moment I felt okay was a sure way to get sick again.

We were regulars at the pediatrician's office, my mother and I. Head colds, upset stomachs, fevers — all warranted a trip to Dr. Goldman's. The receptionist there greeted us with a big hello; I knew my way around the maze of halls and exam rooms. I saw this same doctor year after year, all through my childhood and into my adolescence, feeling awkward — at sixteen — sitting in a waiting room full of sneezing toddlers, my mother right by my side, yellowed copies of *Highlights* magazine fanned out on the end tables. I flipped through the magazines — bored, ashamed, wanting a reason to duck my head — and I solved the puzzles inside. *How many animals are hiding in this jungle? What's wrong with this picture?*

My mother's policy was driven largely by her sense of what was safe and responsible, her belief that the threat of illness was powerful and persistent and needed to be taken into account at all times. When we stepped inside the waiting room at the doctor's office, she wrinkled her nose — in the dry, empty air she saw clouds of viruses and bacteria ready to strike. She lowered herself very carefully into one of the vinyl-cushioned chairs against the wall, as though by not sitting down too hard she could protect herself from the germs dancing on the seat. And she was always commenting on the children in my class who got sent to school with coughs and runny noses. "Her mother should know better," she said on days when she picked me up from school, appalled that Jody was right there swinging on the jungle gym with the rest of us, two parallel tubes of mucus glistening like slugs above her lip. "That child should not be in school today." To her it was a clear sign of neglect, of selfishness: Jody's mother must have had a job that she couldn't take time off from, she must have been too busy with her career to take care of her sick child. Then she told me to wash extra carefully when we got home. She was furious that her own child's health was being compromised.

But there was something else that made my mother so cautious, so quick to usher me into bed, so reluctant to send me back into my routine when I was well again. She missed me as much as I missed her, she enjoyed having me around. And she was proud of the way she managed my care, thankful for the purpose I gave her when I was ill. She knew as well as I did what my sickness did to her, did for her; she was always keeping an eye out for the one thing that made her strong and focused.

My mother not only lifted herself up to ward against illness — proud, elegant, with the certainty of instinct; she also suffered herself, which was its own kind of glory. Sickness connected me to her in this way too: I was following in her path, assuming her legacy. It was a thing she and I shared, the way other mothers and daughters might share a love of classical music, or a passion for baking bread. Sickness was our sweet, sad violin; it was our slow, mysterious rise.

She was constantly battling vague pains, strange symptoms that came and went at will, clusters of complaints that had no theme or organizing principle. She had periods of overwhelming fatigue; she sometimes felt her heart fluttering erratically inside the cage of her ribs like a bird with a broken wing; her fingers got white with cold; a rash bloomed and died around her mouth; her joints ached; her jaw tightened; her head hurt so much she couldn't think; the muscles of her back were in spasm; she was nauseous, dry heaving into the toilet. Her left eye shrank up for an entire year, retreating into the socket of her skull, the lids pulling in the way a bud closes at night — then resumed its original position, more or less matching the right one once again. There were so many reasons for her to stay in bed.

Really it was depression, her body lobbying on her behalf, demanding that she be noticed, and heard. But we didn't call it that. We called it her "malaise," a term one of her many doctors generously gave her. It sounded glamorous to me, like it could be a movie star's perfume, each spray from the bottle heavy and languorous, like a slow fog rolling in.

When my mother was feeling ill, her bedroom was dark — lights out, shades drawn, the paisley pattern illuminated from behind, looking like amoebas in the science films we saw at school — and the door stayed shut. We all had to keep very quiet. If Danny hit me, I cried with my face in my pillow; he and my father couldn't raise their voices; there was no yelling to each other from room to room the way we normally did, no slamming of doors, no screaming. The house was steeped in a tense calm, our usual modes of expression and communication prohibited.

When she needed something, my mother called to my father in a weakened voice. "Ed . . . can you bring me some tea? Ed . . . can you get an ice pack? Ed . . . can you call the doctor? I just can't seem to get rid of this headache." Sometimes she wandered downstairs, taking each shallow step of the staircase with both feet and then slowly coming into the kitchen. "Hi, gang," she would say, wiggling her fingers in our direction, pouting. She squinted against the fluorescent light, her head tilted to the side, as though in defense against an anticipated blow, her voice was a scratch on vinyl.

She did not fast on Yom Kippur, because if she went even half a day without food she was sure to get a migraine. As it was, she symbolically cut back her consumption and still fell sick some years. One Yom Kippur afternoon she was lying in bed, the comforter pulled up around her neck though it was a warm September day, an ice pack across her forehead. A man on a motorcycle kept riding up and down our street, the rumble of his muffler cresting and dying, cresting and dying.

"Doesn't he know?" my mother croaked, sounding insulted. She was talking about Yom Kippur, of course — our neighborhood was predominantly Jewish — but it seemed she was also talking about her migraine. When she was sick she demanded respect. She gained a certain power from the position she put herself in — attacked, victimized. There was something enchanting about her suffering.

She had bottles and bottles of pills lined up on the first two shelves of the medicine cabinet in my parents' bathroom, so many different shapes and colors, so many different doctors prescribing them. Sometimes I opened up the cabinet and looked at them, shook them, held them up to the light, put them back exactly the way I had found them. My mother seemed so important to me, her name typed up in neat black ink on label after label. The vials were like little men in uniform, an army of servants alert, on call, each waiting to perform his own special magic.

I knew that I was one of those pills, something she and I had concocted in our own home lab, more potent than anything an MD could have given her. I was capable of relieving her, of being swallowed.

Eventually, the thing that united my mother and me also pulled us apart. There was a sense of one-upsmanship, there was a kind of unspoken competition. The older I got, the more she retreated into her illnesses, and the more I retreated into mine. The stakes got higher and higher.

My mother stayed in bed for longer stretches, found it harder to get dressed, expanded her circle of prescribing professionals. I was a high school girl who was supposed to be thinking about boys, and sneaking cigarettes, and discovering new territories, flirting with new thresholds, instead of coming back to this same trodden soil. But I turned my back on exploration, growth, life's general bustle, and ran to the safety of old terrain: home ground, my mother's care. I became anorexic, then bulimic, then severely depressed. I had my own medicine men who checked in on me. I slipped into countless hospital johnnies, submitted myself to batteries of tests, answered questions. Time and again, I offered my arm up to a nurse, my veins bulging, blue as the ocean, ready to be drained.

When my mother's parents lived nearby, we used to visit them often. On the windowsill above the kitchen sink in their apartment there was a pill box in the shape of a sparrow. Every time we went over, after kissing my grandparents hello, I would run to look at it. Their house was so filled with strange, enticing things — a sea of Oriental rugs, the odor of mothballs, shelves and shelves of knickknacks, the heavy sounds of German — but it was the sparrow that caught me, surfacing in the darkness of their home the way a door knob glints in the middle of the night. It was gilded, with emerald eyes, its body stamped all around with little hatch marks to represent feathers. Just below the

wings, there was a seam that separated the bird in two. My grandmother would take the sparrow down off the windowsill for me and
open it up. There inside the hollowed-out bottom half was a nest lined
with green felt, filled with a small collection of capsules and tablets,
looking like eggs, containing all of their mystery and promise.

When my grandparents moved to California, my grandmother gave
me the bird. She knew how much I loved it, and besides, she was taking too many medications by then for the sparrow's belly to work; she
had switched to a plastic container with a separate box for each day of
the week. I kept the bird on the second shelf of the bookcase in my
bedroom. It was empty now, of course, but I still liked to open and
close it, letting the two halves lock firmly together. I liked the feel of
the beak against my skin, a dull, hard point; I liked the weight of its
body in my palm. When I was sick I watched the bird from across the
room, its wings neatly folded, its green eyes catching the light, twin-
kling at me.

Looking at that gilded sparrow I knew there was something exotic
about being susceptible and weak, that it could make you special, could
turn a common bird into an exquisite creature. I knew that illness carried with it the charm and mystique of foreign lands, that it meant
freedom, the possibility of flight, a journey to somewhere familiar that
nevertheless felt like escape, the bird itself frail but alluring, delicate
but powerful, its body so easily split in two, its center a chamber from
which to draw cure.

Fade

hen I was a little girl, every day of the week corresponded to a certain color. Sunday was a creamy butter yellow; Monday was the light green of the countertops when we first moved into the house, before my mother redid the kitchen, and it had the same subtle sheen and mottled surface; Tuesday was dusty rose, thick and soft like theater drapes; Wednesday was green again, but darker, deeper, more saturated; Thursday was a fiery red; Friday, chocolate brown; Saturday, black and quiet.

The week was a series of chambers I made my way through, one color bleeding into the next at each threshold. Familiar and surreal: it was both these things. The days meant predictable rhythm; they meant enchantment.

And at night, when I lay in bed with my face mashed into the pillow and my palms pressed into my closed eyes, I saw all kinds of shapes and patterns. Pink paisleys marched across my field of vision. Electric purple swirls wriggled like eels, linked up in a neat grid, and then separated. Bright orange spheres exploded into a thousand shards that floated out in all directions, rained down, and transformed into a rolling wave in the most magnificent blue. I could hardly wait to see what came next. I knew it was an endless parade: all I had to do was press my palms in; there was no danger of running out. I had so much faith.

But then I was nine, ten, eleven, and the colors began to fade out, disappear. The days of the week became ordinary, merely themselves: just Monday and after that Tuesday, no magic or texture. And when I pressed my hands into my eyes in bed at night, there was only brown.

Sometimes I pressed harder, hoping for more, hoping my insistence would bring back the enchantment, jump start the pageant inside my head. It didn't work. The brown refused to change, thick mud that

wouldn't move, but just lay there, and the pressure of my hands created nothing except this: a terrible pain behind my eyes. It made me
think of my mother during one of her sick spells, in her room with an
ice pack against her forehead, a hurt so deep inside.

At camp the summer after I turned twelve, my counselors wrote home
concerned. They said they had heard from staff that I had always been
an excellent camper. But this summer, I was withdrawn. I was isolating myself, brooding; my mood was sour.

They were right. There was a blanket over me, muffling all sensation;
there was a screen between me and the world. I retreated. Everyone
around me seemed stupid, the pattern of our days, worthless. I winced
at the sound of reveille crackling over the PA system; I looked forward
to taps.

On their nights off, our counselors went into town and got drunk,
then came stumbling back in late, banging theirs shins against the metal
frames of our beds, laughing and snorting. Sometimes my cabinmates
woke up and started talking to them. They found our counselors'
slurred speech amusing; they enjoyed the affections that were sloppily
showered upon them. I lay awake in my top bunk bed at the other end
of the room listening, wishing they'd all be quiet so I could get back to
sleep. I wished, too, that I could be like the other girls, who were so
ready for the next adventure, so quick to sit up in their cots and giggle
in the middle of the night, their long hair, released from ponytails for
sleep — twenty brush strokes on one side, twenty on the other —
catching the light of the moon.

One night that summer I had diarrhea in bed — a fart that turned
hot and wet. I was terrified, ashamed, surprised that I could have so
little control, badness leaking out of me. I climbed down from the top
bunk and snuck past the bathroom, past where our cubbies were, out
the back door. Three weathered wood steps, then cold dry grass. I
reached under my nightgown and pulled off my underpants, balled
them up tight, and threw them as far as I could under the cabin, into
the spiderwebs and darkness.

When I got back into bed, I started to wonder whether I had
made a mistake: would the smell of shit rise up through the floor-
boards? Would we all be gagging by morning? Maybe I hadn't thrown
my underpants far enough, maybe the head counselor would see them

when she checked the grounds outside the cabin during inspection the next day.

My parents would have taken care of the situation. I was terribly homesick all summer long, but I missed them especially right then. My mother would have rinsed out my underpants and thrown them in the wash; they would have come out good as new the next day. My father would have said, *It's okay. It happens to everyone; sometimes you just can't tell.* Now my dirty laundry was about to be aired.

But no one ever found out what had happened. In the morning there was sunshine and chatter. There were girls running around brushing their teeth, tying their laces. Inspection was a 9.8: some dust bunnies under one of the beds, a streak on the bathroom mirror.

In a way, it was a bit of a letdown. I saw even more perfectly that there was life tumbling along all around me, and then there was my own private experience. I didn't know how to get past it, how to move to the other side.

I went through the motions. I traded stationery with my cabinmates during rest hour: Holly Hobby for Hello Kitty, Ziggy for Charlie Brown. I joined the swim team. I shrieked and jumped up and down on the dock when the girl before me in the relay race came in to touch the side. I swung the softball bat hard and ran for fly balls. I cheered for my team during Color War.

But always there was a piece of me that stood apart. I couldn't ever forget myself. When I joined the other girls seated cross-legged in the rec hall, watched our counselor's lips along with them as she led us through verse after verse of the blue team's march song, fifty voices singing, I could not lose the sound of my own voice. It came from inside my head, a little bit out of sync, a little bit off key, a separate, singular string of notes fading out as they rose up to the rafters.

Camp, more than any other place I'd been, was supposed to be all about doing — there were activities from sunrise to sunset and you developed team spirit and your life had a soundtrack, Barry Manilow singing all day long on the PA system about Mandy, about making it through the rain — and instead I wandered the edges of that world, encased in my interior self, everything holding me back. And it was in this place, which encouraged the physical — pivot-step-swing, keep-your-eye-on-the-ball, stroke-stroke-turn-your-head-and-breathe —

where it became so clear that my physical self seemed to have lost all importance and receded. I was a petite girl with suntanned skin, braces, dry elbows, no signs yet of hips or waist, only the tiniest mosquito-bite breasts. But in the distorted, schematic image that I had developed, I was this: an enormous head, cumbersome, misshapen, sitting atop a withered body.

In my mind I looked like one of the pinkish creatures my cabin-mates and I had found on a nature walk in the woods behind the camp. They were nearly see-through, propelling themselves around a shallow pool, big heads first, brittle, fragile bodies trailing behind. They looked prehistoric; we thought we had discovered some unknown species.

"Oh, those?" our counselor laughed, after we dragged her over to take a look. "Those are just crayfish!"

The world had turned into a dull place, where everything was ordinary, full of disappointment.

Ants

very year for their anniversary, my mother presented my father with another piece of Winston Churchill memorabilia. One year it was a photograph, the next year a marble figurine. This year it was a new biography. The three of us were standing in the kitchen; the big, rectangular fluorescent light was a canopy over our heads. My brother never seemed to be around for these formal moments, these presentations: his cards were a last-minute affair, something scribbled on loose-leaf paper and slipped under my parents' bedroom door just before midnight, a few words and a hastily sketched-out gift certificate for some quality time with their son, or an IOU for a week of picking up after himself with no reminders.

My father turned the book over a couple of times, thumbed through the pages.

"Hey, that's great," he said. Then he went into the living room to place the newest addition to the collection on the Churchill wall.

My father presented my mother with an antique pin.

"Very nice," she said, nodding. She cupped it in her palm as if it were a small toad, its ruby eyes glowing. "Very nice." Then it disappeared into her jewelry box.

They gave each other an anniversary kiss. They puckered up big, the touch was minimal. It looked like a cartoon peck, where the lovers' lips stretch out across a vast, blank expanse to meet each other with a loud, wet smack. Except that here the posture showed not the distance they were willing to travel in order to make contact, but the force with which their bodies instinctively pulled them apart.

I presented them with a handmade card in which I'd inscribed an original rhyme: "To the best couple in the world by far, whether at home or in the car. You two folks were meant to be, that's something anyone can plainly see."

They laughed, they admired the cleverness of the rhyme. My mother reached out to touch the back of my father's head. His hand flew up to smooth down the hair that she'd ruffled as though he were about to swat a mosquito. Then — as if on second thought — he patted her shoulder, gave it a quick squeeze. Every time he touched her, it was a concession.

"Okay, terrific," she said, smiling. "This was just great." We stood there blinking at each other. Then my mother started to load the dishwasher.

It seemed there were always two levels. There was the thing that you wished were happening, the thing you might even see if you looked quickly enough, and then, underneath, there was the thing that was really going on.

When I was a small child, my mother and I were browsing in an antique store run by an old woman with a mist of gray hair. As we were getting ready to leave, the old woman offered me a plate of chocolate chip cookies.

Just as I was about to put the first cookie in my mouth, I noticed some tiny ants crawling around on it.

"I can't eat it," I said. "It has ants."

"Oh, no," the woman said, chuckling. "Those aren't ants, dear, those are chocolate *chips*."

My mother laughed with her.

"No, thank you," I said, lifting the cookie up toward her. "There are ants all over it."

"What an imagination!" my mother said. Then she turned to the old woman. "If she won't eat, she won't eat." She shrugged her shoulders as if to say, *Aren't kids strange?*

But there were ants on the cookie, I saw them moving, I saw their tiny legs traversing the rocky surface. They were there, invisible except to me, a frenzy of dashes, bumping into each other, wandering blindly, picking up crumbs.

Unspoken

could tell by the first period of the first day at my new school that Julie Prince was the most popular girl. We were assembled in the gym, and there she was, somehow the focus amid one hundred and thirty kids, as though a spotlight from the bleachers had been trained on her: a swarm of girls around her, a few bold boys swaggering up to talk. Her face was tan skin, a big smile, bright blue eyes. She had a real figure, she wore jeans that were faded to the perfect shade, purple feather earrings hung at her jaw.

I had never seen feather earrings before.

It was seventh grade, a secular private school. My parents had decided to pull me out of my Jewish day school the year before, after I had reported that if there was a question in science class, it was quite common for our teacher to excuse herself to go to the bathroom, bringing the textbook with her. A religious education was important, but so was learning about the solar system: my parents wanted me to fit in everywhere. My mother marveled happily at my "WASP calves" — she equated well-defined muscles with access to mainstream society. My father was already taking me to the Harvard Club and teaching me to play squash because racquet sports were "social sports" — they helped you make friends, they made you a viable entity. And afterward, when we sat at the bar sipping Cokes, he would ask me to watch carefully what was going on around us. "This is how people network, you see," he would say. "This is how deals get made." My parents wanted all of that for me; they wanted me to be well rounded, get into a top college, succeed.

I could have gone to the Orthodox school where Danny was starting eleventh grade — the secular education there was apparently good enough — but I chose this school instead. The decision had nothing to do with religion. Danny's school was in the heart of Manhattan, and

I wanted a campus with fields and trees and a stone wall kids could sit on between classes.

I sat on that wall, sometimes, but mostly I sat alone that year, studying Julie Prince and all the other sophisticated twelve-year-old girls. They seemed like foreign creatures to me, so at home in the world. They moved with a confidence I had lost; their speech was sprinkled with references I did not get. They listened to music I had never heard of. They dressed well. They went to the movies with boys on Friday nights, went shopping together without their parents on Saturday afternoons — that's what you could do if you were a city kid, if you didn't observe Shabbat, if your world didn't revolve around your parents, if you didn't sense that for all their talk about social success, they needed you to stay exactly where you were, if you were not terrified of growing up and leaving them.

I stayed home with my parents on Fridays and Saturdays. At night we watched television. We had it set to a timer so we wouldn't be violating Shabbat: off at midnight Friday, on again Saturday at four. We called the timer a *shabbos* clock, as though giving it this name made it a facet of our religious observance. We couldn't change the channel — touching the television was taboo — so we were stuck with the lineup of whatever network we chose, passively waiting for each time slot to end, for the next show's credits to come on.

Danny often spent the weekend with friends in the city. If he was home, he stayed in his room, playing chess with imaginary components, working out math problems in his head. When the *shabbos* clock came on, he camped in front of the television. The weekends he was with us, I could feel his presence in the house, a sustained tension. He wasn't doing his schoolwork. His essays and reports were subpar, if they were turned in at all. His status at school was in jeopardy, and there was the prospect of college looming ahead: how would he ever get in? There were fights, ultimatums, doorjambs broken by so much slamming.

And yet still, weekends seemed to pass so quietly, with so much still unspoken; the days had a muffled, muted feel, as though we were all encased in glass and I was watching us from the other side. I went to *shul* with my father; I sat reading in the den with my mother for hours, she with her sagas from the library, I with my school books, and sometimes *Seventeen*, whose pages I combed trying to figure out how to be more like Julie. My parents fought with gestures and cold shoulder treatments; they mimed their frustration, their rage. Meals were devoured quickly, with almost no conversation. We walked around the house barefoot, or in slippers. The grandfather clock ticked away.

On Sundays the three of us took trips to the Berkshires to look for a country house, my father smiling at the scenery the whole way up, one hand on the steering wheel, the other hand painting the air in front of him with tiny strokes. Though they could never agree on what they wanted, my parents were enthusiastic about the prospect of a country house.

"It'll be just great," my father said. "A family retreat, a place where the whole gang can spend time together." And yet it seemed that my entire life was a family retreat; imagining more togetherness was terrifying. I thought of us isolated in the country, a squat New England house on snow-covered acres, the nearest neighbor half a mile away, gray clouds puffing out of our brick chimney like smoke signals, an SOS.

But I could not undo the scene in my head either, could not replace it with an alternative. I was a lonely girl: I wanted friends, I wished for some other life beyond my own. I felt everything pressing in on me, a pressure inside me equally strong, straining my bones, tweaking my nerves, it was something big, and yet —

I didn't really want out. I had learned that life was not about what I wanted deep within; I had learned the lesson so well I had no idea what was really wrong. Sometimes I felt a little bit like screaming, but I could not imagine what words might spill off my tongue, or recognize what caused the tickle of fury so far down inside me, or figure out where my voice should direct itself, and so an outburst did not seem justified. And the tightness I felt — that vague and terrible pressure — was reassuring, in a way. My life was in balance, and balance had its own allure. There was a corridor of emptiness between my parents, but it was an emptiness I could fill. I could do cartwheels down that corridor, I could paint its walls in the most glorious colors, and they could smile. I gave my mother purpose, I gave my father friendship; I gave them my good self, my complete self, while my brother gave them trouble. This was what I knew, it was how things had always been, it made my parents happy. How could I turn away from that?

So when my mother suggested that it might be nice for me to invite friends up to stay with me at the country house we were still looking to buy, I could not insert someone from school into that context; there was no room for anyone else in the picture. It was family, an impermeable, immutable knot.

To get to school, I carpooled with some other kids from my town. While everyone else climbed into one of several big yellow buses that headed back into Manhattan, I walked slowly toward whichever car happened to be waiting in front of the breezeway that day. Another mark of difference; I was full of shame. The worst was when it was my mother's turn to pick up. She always got there early and sat watching the other seventh graders mill around. She was on the lookout, as fascinated as I was. If her malaise was acting up, she had her down coat pulled over a pair of sweats. Sometimes she wore her slippers; sometimes her hair was flattened on one side. I hoped no one could see through the glass.

"Who's that girl over there?" she would ask me when I got into the car. "She looks sweet." Or: "Who was that boy who said good-bye to you?" Or: "Look at those girls giggling by the door — don't they look like they're having fun?"

I would glance over, following her gaze. And it was true, they did look like they were having fun, their heavy book bags dropped like boulders at their feet, their hands flapping, flipping their hair, twisting their earrings, their laughter carrying across the breezeway. But it was my job to notice them, to watch and wonder. I couldn't stand my mother's desperation, how it mirrored my own. I buckled up my seat belt, sank down low against the door, waited for the car to fill up so we could finally take off.

My father and brother came home from the city late in the evening, so my mother and I often had dinner alone, and she would ask me to tell her about school, her voice so full of anxiety, her eyes searching my face with such intensity, that I was almost afraid to speak. I could see she was waiting for me to proudly report to her that I had a whole slew of friends, and school was like a party, and could I please be excused, I had several dozen phone calls to make. I felt crowded out in those moments; I had the sense that she was sitting right next to me, our thighs touching, her own downy skin catching the steam that rose from my plate, though in reality she was on the other side of the table.

"Well," I would begin, "in math class today — "

"In math class what?" she would say, if I paused for the slightest second. "What happened in math class?"

And then I could no longer tell her what had happened in math class: the words had no room to come out.

Sometimes I wonder if this is why I write: because there is room, finally, in these pages, for the words to come out, and because I still yearn for that gentle listener who was missing from my life for so long, each string of black letters like one more delicate chain that will link us together in experience, you and I.

Of course, what I say is different now, I am not telling you about the incident in math class; I am telling you, I think, about more important things. My mother has given me a stronger voice, with much to offer — her own unwitting gift, something I am thankful for.

But then, it was a different gift she wanted me to have, and it was not hers to give. She wanted me to have a social life, yet she could not see it as something that might blossom on its own, without her interference — which was really a way to stay connected. She could not see that her interference was hindering its growth, making me reluctant to strike out in a way that was wholly mine, to create an existence on my own, something I might be entitled to hold onto.

Julie Prince was in my social studies class. It was strange to be in such proximity to her and to feel how far apart we really were. I could not help glancing over at her during class. I wanted to look at her face, her jewelry. I wanted to see how she crossed her legs, how she held her pen, the doodles she made in the margins when she wasn't paying attention. She was not a good student, she didn't seem to care very much about school, and I wanted to know what that was like, too: how you could just disregard assignments because you'd rather be flirting with a boy, how you could not try your hardest, how you could show up to class just in the nick of time, your homework a mess, or maybe not done at all, how you could feel the world was yours anyway, there was nothing you had to earn, nothing you had to worry about.

One Friday in the middle of the school year, Julie came to class a few minutes into the period, officially late. Mr. Arnold was talking about the map of Africa, how we had to learn all the countries, how we were citizens of the world. Instead of heading to her seat at the far end of the room, Julie walked up to Mr. Arnold's desk and stopped, close but not that close, as though they were both actors on stage, the whole class assembled and watching, an audience.

Except that when it came time to speak her lines, she couldn't.

Something had happened to her during lunch. It was as though her tongue had swelled to fill up her whole mouth and her throat had tightened up and the words just wouldn't come out. She sounded a bit like a deaf person when she tried to talk, her voice all up and down the register, her syllables thick, unclipped. She stuck her head out with the strain of trying to force out the words. She clutched her throat.

"I hit my head," she managed to explain. "I can't talk."

There was laughter at first, and even Mr. Arnold was smiling, but then the laughter died into silence and Mr. Arnold's face turned dark. He looked concerned; he sent her to the nurse's office.

I was mesmerized. It was scary and wonderful to watch Julie struggle, to see her breezy demeanor, which I had come to rely on, replaced by awkwardness and panic. In those few moments, it seemed that we were all on the brink of something big; I suddenly believed everything could change — for better or worse, I didn't know; all I felt was possibility. I was connected to Julie right then. I saw her vulnerability. I understood that something was caught inside of her, that she was blocked, confused. I saw that she was trying to dredge up a voice that could communicate; I knew how difficult an enterprise that was.

But when Julie came to class the following Monday she was fine. I never heard anyone say anything about the episode, which began to seem like something I might have imagined. And in my mind it became further evidence of the divide between her world and mine, further proof of her inaccessibility, her perfection. Those struggling syllables, her language stretched and straining, all of it was hers. It was something she had rendered lovely, something we did not share. She wore feather earrings, her lips were coated with the shiny gloss you could find only at a certain counter at Bloomingdale's that I had heard some girls make reference to. She spoke in tongues.

I studied from the time I got home until I went to bed. When I took my bath at night, my mother sat on the edge of the tub and quizzed me on vocabulary, on Spanish verbs, on the periodic table. The night before an exam, she made fish for dinner.

"It's brain food," she said. "It'll help you."

And maybe it did. I was an excellent student. I did all my work on time, I got good grades. I obeyed all the rules with great care. In English class, we had to write an eight-hundred-word letter to a friend, and I counted the words, one by one, crossing out, adding, until I had the number right, then copied the whole thing over onto stationery. I wrote the letter to a girl from camp; for the assignment, I pretended she was a friend. There was no one else I could think of to write to. The letter was pitifully boring, full of the specifics of my day. It contained nothing unexpected, nothing of my interior life, the thoughts that moved so deep inside they weren't really thoughts at all, the feelings that surfaced and caught the light but then disappeared before I could name them.

My English teacher said there would be a test on *One Day in the Life of Ivan Denisovich*, she said we had to know that book inside and out, and I read and reread, and took elaborate notes on the plot, until I could tell you what Ivan Denisovich had for lunch and dinner that day, who he talked to and in what order, the work details he was assigned to.

At the time, I didn't know that plot is the key to the treasure, not the treasure itself; I didn't know that action yielded something deeper, contained a code that might be worth cracking. I didn't understand that lives could be read in different ways, that there was such a thing as perspective, the freedom to see things a certain way, to describe the view from where you stood, no matter how bad the angles were, how ugly the trees, how heavy the sky.

At the time, it was so important to do the right thing; there were so many instructions to be followed.

At parent-teacher conferences, my teachers said I was too well behaved.

"I wish just one of these days that I would catch her with the back of her head facing me," said Mr. Arnold. "I wish she would whisper to the girl behind her, get into trouble every once in a while."

"Let her join the field hockey team when she gets to high school," my advisor told them. "Let her get out some of that pent up aggression, let her whack at some other girls' shins."

But when ninth grade came along, I didn't join the field hockey team; I joined the gymnastics team instead. Gymnastics was all about poise and grace, aggression contained and channeled instead of set loose. You charged the vault, feet pounding against the wood floor, and all that momentum took you into the air, knees locked, toes pointed. You tumbled across the mat, whipping your body around, picking up speed, and still you danced, pert little steps, a smile on your face, ponytail swinging merrily from side to side.

And during practice, your coach stood nearby in her shiny striped sweats and yelled at you to *drive* those legs around faster, leap higher, pound that springboard harder.

Your hips got puffy from banging so many times against the bottom parallel bar, the flesh somehow both sensitive and numb, your shins began to ache from sprinting on the gym floor, and the callouses you got on your palms from gripping and swinging around wood eventually ripped, revealing patches of stinging skin — wet, raw, the color of raspberries, so tender it was impossible to touch.

I was never very good at gymnastics, and I got worse when the pressure was on. I hated practice, hated the meets. I was miserable, but I could not quit. I was not a quitter; quitting was wrong: it disappointed people, it meant you were weak.

But sometimes the body has ways of speaking for you, of saying what needs to be said even before you really understand that something must be spoken. Every afternoon during my second year on the team, my throat began to swell up, and by the time practice came, there was a lump so big I had to hunch my shoulders to swallow. My neck felt huge to me; it throbbed. Sometimes the pain was so bad I could excuse myself from practice. But when I looked in the mirror at home, there was nothing. And by nighttime, the pain had disappeared completely. My mother thought allergies, my coach thought I was making it up. I thought I was just plain sick. Now I think it was a yell caught deep inside, trying to surface; it was the ghost of an awful scream.

Compare/Contrast

Here is what happened when my father's father died:

My grandfather's body was sent from Florida up to New York for burial.

During the funeral service, I couldn't stop sobbing, though no one else seemed to be — not even my father, his brother, or my grandmother — and I hardly knew my grandfather myself. I was thirteen years old.

I did not go to the cemetery. I was told it would be too upsetting. While everyone else was burying my grandfather, my mother's friend Lynne took me out for ice cream a few blocks from the funeral home. I was not hungry, it was only eleven in the morning, and it was an unseasonably chilly May day, too cold for ice cream anyway, but I got a three-scoop dish.

The *shiva* was at our house — visitors trickling in and out for the week, carrying baskets full of bagels, trays of deviled eggs, bowls of whitefish salad. In accordance with the rules of mourning, my father stayed in the house, the mirrors were covered, he did not put on shoes. He remained unshaven for thirty days.

For the next eleven months, he went to synagogue services every morning and every evening to say Kaddish. He did not do things that could be construed as celebration — going to the movies, entertaining guests, attending United Jewish Appeal dinners. He pulled away from the world during this period; at the same time, something essential was drawn out of him. He was like an old photograph of himself: two-dimensional, fading.

I gave him the leeway he needed. I sat with him in silence in the backyard, in front of the television, at the breakfast room table. I let his sadness envelop me.

Eleven days after my father's father died, my mother's father died. Here is what happened then:

The morning after we got the news, I blurted out over breakfast: "Boy, they sure are dropping like flies." My parents found this amusing.

I could not locate any feelings of sadness or grief. I was not close to this grandfather, either, but I experienced his death as the death of a stranger. I did not cry.

The funeral took place in California, where my grandfather died. My parents did not buy me a plane ticket. I was told that traveling now would be too disruptive for me, and I should study for my final exams instead. I spent the next week at my mother's friend Lynne's house.

My father returned after a week, my mother, after two weeks. For the next month or so she carried balled up tissues in her pocket wherever she went. There was a chance that whatever she was saying would dissolve in a wash of big tears that pooled up in her eyes, adding luster to the deep brown of her irises, before sliding down her cheeks. During this period of time, her whole face seemed fluid, quivery, like what you see in the distance on the highway in the middle of a hot summer day.

I was put off by her susceptibility to collapse: it struck me as unfair, after all the times she had asked me to snap out of it, to paste a quick smile on my face. Her sadness seemed weak, histrionic, a campaign for the spotlight, while my father grieved in private — so much more modestly and elegantly but also with so much more of a burden: he had to support her during her breakdowns, let her cry against his shoulder, put his own mourning on hold. What I didn't see was that this was also, on some level, his preference. He participated; he had some choice. He was not only responding but initiating. The push came from both sides; they balanced each other out.

I kept my distance from my mother during this period, as though her tears were a toxic substance, a fluid that might contaminate me.

Decorating Tips

hen I was in high school, my father sometimes came into my room and just stood there, looking around. He let his eyes mist up; he did not try to conceal a proud grin. I would be on my bed studying, books and notebooks fanned out around me.

"I tell ya," he would say to me, "I just love this room. It says exactly who you are."

Every time he told me this I felt a change in pressure in the air, my breath sucked out of my lungs a bit, my organs compressed, something tightening across my body, quick and violent.

This is what my room looked like:

- three walls papered in a print of kelly green, bright yellow, and white — clusters of flowers with big droopy petals and short, rigid stems.
- the fourth wall and the ceiling covered in a different wallpaper: daisies outlined in sky blue, with buttons of apple green at the center.
- a circular shag rug in the exact green, yellow, and white of the wallpaper.
- drapes and bedspread in the exact pattern of the green, yellow, and white wallpaper.
- yellow furniture, including two sets of bookcases filled with stuffed animals.
- two kelly green bulletin boards, with a random assortment of items tacked to them: fading ribbons from track meets at camp, old theater tickets and Playbills, a couple of birthday cards, a

photograph or two of friends; all in all, there was not much, and a lot of the green was still visible.

It was a room that had not changed since I was five.

I didn't know why, all those years living in that house, I never did anything different to my room, why I made only half-hearted attempts to keep the bulletin boards up to date, occasionally tacking up a new photograph, never taking down what was already there. I didn't know why I never removed the bulletin boards altogether — they were my father's idea — and hung a Simon and Garfunkel poster in their place, or the big gauzy tapestry that I had bought at a flea market one summer in Israel, why I didn't roll up the shag rug and leave the floor bare, throw the stuffed animals in a box, politely suggest to my mother that it was time to redecorate.

It was not as though the rest of the house had remained exactly the same: the armchair in the living room had been reupholstered, the den had been wallpapered and outfitted with a new modular couch, my parents' bathroom had been retiled, a new sink and toilet installed, all the fabrics and patterns and models pulled from the shopping bag overflowing with swatches and magazine ads that my mother had collected over the years. Each minor change was like a logjam on a river coming undone, water flowing easily again; it was a reminder that nothing is fixed, really, that even houses can grow.

But my room stayed the same; it did not get redecorated, though the girls I had started to make friends with had all gone through this — at thirteen, fourteen, fifteen — their mothers helping them pick out a nice Laura Ashley wallpaper, feminine but also sophisticated, some Marimekko bedding with bold blocky patterns, 'a freestanding full-length mirror in one corner of the room, a new desk to accommodate the typewriter, the increased workload at school. It was almost a rite of passage.

I visited my friend Eileen's house when her room was in the middle of being redone — a present for her fourteenth birthday — the paint smelling so fresh, so full of possibility, the new Laura Ashley sheets cool and soft, white cotton with lavender dots. It turned out that Eileen stained those sheets a couple of months later, sleeping too soundly, her period running thick and fast in the middle of the night. She was upset but also amused by the incident. She laughed hard telling the story, and I admired her reaction — it seemed somehow alive and open — but there was a part of me that was horrified, too, by the force of her body, the way it behaved in such an unruly manner, leaving stains that would not come out. I had no idea how I would respond if it happened to me: my sheets were old sheets and I was still waiting — then, and at fifteen, sixteen, seventeen — waiting in the most casual, uninterested way, for my first period.

That first period. Its absence was something, in the very beginning; we — my mother and I — were expecting it to come. For a while, there was a sense of anticipation, excitement, but also, for me, great mystery. How did it happen, exactly? Was it like a faucet turned on just to the point where the drips became a slim string of liquid? Or did it come and go in bursts? Could you feel the blood coming out? These questions occurred to me at night when I was lying in bed, but I was too embarrassed to ask my mother or anyone else.

My mother went out and bought some maxipads.

"I'm putting them right here in the linen closet," she told me, "on this shelf, okay, Deb? Behind the soaps. So when the time comes . . ."

And I kept guessing the time had come. Whenever I felt something squeeze out of me, I rushed to the bathroom, expecting to see a dot of blood, a trace of pink, finding nothing.

When I went away to gymnastics camp for the summer after eighth grade, my mother packed the pads in my suitcase. In August, I came home, and there they were still: shiny plastic packaging pulled tight around them, intact. A quiet failure; also a small sense of relief.

As time passed, the relief grew. I began not to care at all — I began to be thankful, even — that my period had not yet come. I didn't wonder, *When? When?* Instead, I thought, *Good.* In my mind, the relief had nothing to do with the risk of pregnancy; sex was something I was still only dimly aware of, and certainly not actively pursuing. In my mind, it had to do with the body on its own — it was almost an aesthetic consideration. Over the years, one by one, the girls around me had crossed over into a new place: full of messes, dark and out of control. I started to feel a little superior when I heard stories like Eileen's, and there were so many! I was missing out on this experience where I was, but I was also safe. Safe.

I had developed like everyone else on the outside — my breasts were average size, my hips were beginning to show themselves, my waist was sucking itself in — but inside I was different; even, I thought, even special. There was something so clean and graceful about me, something ordered. I pictured my organs resting in place, shiny like the shoes lined up side by side in my closet, behaving perfectly, inert.

When I was fifteen, my mother said, "Now, remember, I was a late starter, too."

She said, "Let me show you how to put in a tampon," as though it were simply lack of preparation that was causing the delay. Again, she told me, "So when the time comes . . ."

I was curious about the way that tampons worked, and besides, I felt that in this demeaning exercise there was a point I wanted to prove: I was not ready for any of this; it was beyond me. So I agreed to try the tampon. I lay on my back on the bed in the guest room — for some reason, my mother and I were in the guest room, as if we both knew my bedroom couldn't allow such behavior — and poked for a while with the tip of the tampon. I made my mother go into the bathroom.

From behind the door she started reminiscing. "You know, Deb," she told me, "when I was in my twenties, already married to Dad, I called the gynecologist in a panic in the middle of the night. I had gone to the bathroom to take out my tampon and I couldn't find the string. I thought it was lost somewhere inside of me." She laughed. "Can you believe how little I knew?" She paused. "You know — don't you? — that that can't happen." Then she got more focused. "Just push," she told me. "Just ease it in."

But the tampon was dry and scratchy, and the opening of my vagina felt that way too. I tried and tried, but it hurt, a sharp sting, flesh about to tear. I didn't want to be doing this anymore; it seemed obscene, a violation I was committing against myself. I gave up; I rested my case. There was a dew of perspiration all over my body; the hair at my temples had frizzed. I examined the tampon: it pushed out of its cardboard casing, the cotton head now a little fuzzy, untidy. I held it up to my nose: it smelled like the worst of me.

A little while after that incident, something funny happened. My mother and I both forgot about my period. When I went away on trips, she stopped putting pads in my suitcase. Perhaps she was tired of waiting; perhaps she had had second thoughts: she loved me so much, why not hold onto me forever? Danny was away at college, and with all the distracting energy his presence had introduced now gone, the distance between my parents had become more pronounced. My mother dragged herself through the days in a pair of sweatpants. During the week, my father often stayed at the apartment they had bought in Manhattan. She and I were alone together so much; I was there for her.

I was in my safe clean place, where I went about my business: studying hard, writing papers, learning my Latin declensions. There were PSATs and SATs and achievement tests you had to do well on. There were advanced placement classes. There was fish for dinner many nights.

Sometimes I raged. I called my mother a bitch. I told her to get a life, leave me alone, stop being so pushy, let me breathe. I screamed and screamed. I thought, sometimes, that I might kill her, the anger was so big. Instead I threw my hardcover textbooks against the wall, my heaviest shoes. I broke the doorjambs that my brother had not gotten to. It was as though, with him gone from the house, I had to play both roles to keep things in balance, or maybe his absence gave me more space to do what needed to be done.

But my mother never fought back, never told me what she was feeling, never brought herself into the argument. She cried, she looked wounded — this much I could sometimes elicit from her — but then she disappeared. She left the room, left me standing there with my fury and frustration and disappointment, not knowing where to put any of it. And the next thing I knew she was offering to make me a sandwich, or drive me to the store for some new clothing, and it was as though nothing had happened, as though I hadn't spoken up at all, as though half an hour earlier I hadn't come this close to digging my fingers into the flesh of her neck.

And my father, who had once been my ally, who had defended me, who had demanded I be allowed to cry when my mother insisted I smile, who also experienced her presence as a suffocating pressure, a choking out of air and light, began to shift his allegiance when he saw that I was no longer just a vulnerable child but a monster with teeth, with fingernails.

"Mom means well," he would say to me, no matter how much she had interfered in my life, no matter how much of my being she was demanding. "You have to be nicer to her."

After a time, I gave up. I disappeared too. It hardly seemed worth it to fight. Fighting made my vocal chords ache, my voice hoarse. And for what?

The issue of my period came up occasionally — for example, when I saw the pediatrician, who said it was something to keep an eye on. Yes, I was still going to the pediatrician, my mother took me there, and though I felt funny in that office, I could not think of somewhere else I should be going; I didn't complain. And here is one important point: despite the initial flurry of preparation for the arrival of my period, we all still thought of me as a little girl, a girl who didn't go to gynecologists, a girl who belonged in a room full of stuffed animals and bright flowers.

Who knows whether the body responds to what the brain is telling it, or if all of this is just coincidence? The girl who was afraid of growing up, the girl who was not really expected to grow up, was a girl who didn't get her period. Who knows whether a wish alone can halt the body's progress?

It was in the genes, perhaps: my mother had told me she was late herself. But I had inherited other things from her, too: a need to keep the body at bay, under control, a need to be organized, through and through.

And there is something else I might want to mention. When I was sixteen, I stopped eating for a little while, and then the next year I started throwing up my food, on and off for the rest of high school, and the research shows that anorexia and bulimia will mess with your reproductive system, delaying the onset of menses, but I feel I cannot talk about that here. It is a separate story, though of course it really isn't, it is all part of the same story. Maybe the illness is the story I have been telling all along, maybe I am the story it has been telling, but it thinks of itself as separate, that is its point, in a way: to be a location, almost, we can even call it a room, where bad things are stored behind a shut door.

Behind the shut door of my room, I sat on my bed feeling trapped, stifled, as though the temperature were always a hundred degrees and there were no windows, staring at the flowers on my walls. I wanted to pluck them one by one, let the moisture slowly seep out of them — they were so full of wetness and droop! — let them shrivel up and blow away. But I resisted the urge to try out fresh colors and patterns, which is also the impulse toward fresh textures of experience. I resisted because it was scary; when you redecorate you destroy, too. It is a violent process, really: paper gets torn down in jagged sheets, furniture gets thrown away, layers of wall drop down in slivers, the paint flakes off like snow, and you lose the portrait of yourself: the girl in the three-paneled mirror that sits on top of a yellow dresser, a background of blue-edged daisies. It is the portrait that we had all come to rely on. So much — too much — was at risk.

Still, there was a part of me that yearned. I told myself that in this house, my parents' house, there would never be a room that said exactly who I was, that it was simply not possible. I told myself that I was biding my time here, riding it out, though I was disappointed in myself for not being bolder, more decisive, less complicitous. I hung on by dreaming of another room, which was truly my own room, somewhere else, someplace I would get to soon enough.

I dreamed of that other room, and yet it was an unfinished image. The floor was a blond wood, the walls were unpapered; they were painted white, or peach, or perhaps a very pale blue. This much I was clear on. But I had no idea how I would decorate the room that said who I really was, or where I would put it. When I pictured it, it was not attached to anything, there was no particular view — no rainy city street to look down upon, black umbrellas bumping into each other, no forest with deer charging through. And the room itself was entirely empty. There was no furniture; there was nothing on the walls; there were no soft rugs or billowing drapes. There was just a window with sun streaming in and a misshapen square of light on the floor.

When I was seventeen, a junior in high school, I was sent, finally, to an endocrinologist, who could find nothing wrong with my hormones, and a gynecologist, who told me my reproductive system looked just fine. I began a course of hormone therapy because this is what the doctor told me to do, and I had always been a very good patient, and a month later, I got my period. It didn't feel like a milestone; it didn't feel like a part of me. It was just something that had happened to my body, artificially induced, a staged incident that nonetheless now required a bit of management, like a hangnail, a sprained toe. It was springtime, and the tulips in my neighborhood looked like paper cups; the daffodils: melting plastic.

Also in the spring, I decided to move my twin bed so that instead of sticking straight out into the center of the room, it ran lengthwise against the daisy-papered wall. This was the extent of change I was willing or able to make, and it seemed monumental, or I made it so. *I was so tired of having the bed that way!* I told myself, surveying the room from my new perspective. *Here*, I told myself, *here is much, much better.*

Lying in my bed one night soon after that, I noticed that the wallpaper was lifting at the seam right by my head. Unsure of what had inspired me, not knowing what I'd do next, I peeled a little bit of the paper off in a spiral and then left the strip hanging from the wall. It looked like a ringlet of hair. I grabbed a blue ballpoint pen from my desk and drew a face on the exposed circle of wall, no bigger than a nickel, yellow-brown from the paper's dried glue. It was the kind of face a child would draw. Two dots for the eyes, an upside-down *U* for the nose, and a squiggly line for the mouth. The head of a girl in a field full of daisies. The expression: half grimace, half smile.

No Man's Land

t was a Friday night, my junior year of high school, and I sat studying for the SATs. Since I could not write on Shabbat, I used tiny chips of Planter's peanuts instead of a pencil to fill in the bubbles on the practice tests. The peanut chips were nearly weightless and prone to sliding; one false move and all my answers were jumbled. I had to be very careful.

I was at the dining room table of our apartment in New York City, where we stayed on weekends. My father, who was there all week, would have preferred to go back to the suburbs Friday afternoon, but my friends were in the city, and he was happy to sacrifice the quiet, the fresh air, the backyard on my behalf. We had started spending weekends in New York soon after my parents bought the apartment the previous year, when it was in the middle of major renovations and there were no beds, no mirrors, no dishes in the custom-built cabinets. That's how intent my parents were on turning me into a better-adjusted teenager; that's how invested they were in the enterprise. They were tricky that way, managing to stick right there with me during the process of breaking away, so it became a shared vision, a mutual campaign, and therefore not much like breaking away at all.

I had made friends at school, finally. They were not part of what I used to think of as the popular group, which no longer interested me. They were part of a segment that had not initially registered: funny, sensitive, driven; a little bit weird. They had slowly emerged from a crowd and revealed themselves, just as I must have revealed myself to them. We had found each other.

But when I was at home in the suburbs during the week, or there in our tiny apartment on weekends, these friends seemed to belong to some other world. I felt disconnected, left behind — as though I had been plucked from a conveyer belt that they were continuing to ride and would have to race to catch up with them again the next time I saw them. I always had the sense that I was missing out.

For example, I had no idea what my friends were doing just then, while I was placing my peanuts down on a sheet of paper, unable to use the phone, to take the bus, to eat dinner out. Beth might be drinking red wine at Alexandra's house and flirting with Sam. Ethan and Eileen might have gone to the new Woody Allen movie. Something funny and memorable might be happening, something scandalous. From where I sat I could hear the noises of the street — the horns, the sirens, the doormen's whistles; everyone going, going — but the city was only an abstract thought to me, not something alive and pulsing three floors down.

The real SATs were scheduled for a Saturday morning the following month. Afterward, my friends would hug each other with relief and compare their answers and celebrate by tearing up their notes and getting high. I would take the test the Sunday after that, at my brother's high school, in a room full of similarly observant Jews whom I had never seen before.

Shabbat had once been a space I entered into. It was an arena in which my parents did battle, yes, but it was also a quiet zone outside of weekday life, like a cave you might slip inside, damp and dark and soothing, with textured walls and a soft, soft floor. Special rules guided my behavior, made me so clearly a part of my family, told me who I was. I spent long days with my mother and father; I couldn't think of a better way to pass the time. We were in it together, our own little world.

Lately I had begun to think of Shabbat as something that stood in my way, making demands I no longer wanted to honor. When the sun went down on Friday night, I was forced to retreat, while my friends went about the work of being teenagers: collecting on street corners like vampires brought to life by darkness, looking for risk and fun, for experience.

Shabbat was the time my parents were in the house together the most, and I sat watching them, transfixed: the sighs and shrugs, my father's resigned chuckle, my mother's aggressive refusal to listen. I watched the way each of them pulled in and stiffened — an animal response to threat — when touched by the other: my father's hands on my mother's shoulders, or her fingers coaxing a stray hair back into place on his head. Their marriage was on the verge of collapse, should have collapsed long ago except they believed in "sticking it out," no matter how incompatible they were, no matter how miserable doing so made them. They lived that way, keeping their distance, turning away from each other at night, their twin beds pushed together but made with separate sheets.

The tension between them was something I couldn't help picking up and couldn't distract myself from, though I tried to focus on other things: the fraying edge of the quilt that hung on the wall, the flatness of my stomach, the bulb on the awning of the apartment building across the avenue going red, a cab's wheels squealing to a stop in response.

Shabbat was the time when my father and I talked the most: he needed a best friend so badly, a woman he could share his life with, and I was that woman, though I was really just a girl of sixteen. He wanted to know how I liked the painting reproduced in the *New York Times* that day, and whether I had ever dreamed of traveling to Alaska, and what my friends and I talked about when we went out for dinner. The comparisons to my mother weaved their way into our conversations, too, and so did all his complaints and regrets, his anger and disappointment.

He looked around the apartment — the walls, the carpet, the furniture, everything the color of sand — and whispered his dissatisfaction to me.

"I would have wanted something bolder, you see, some patterns, some accents, *something*. But Mom," he said, shaking his head, "Mom just doesn't — "

"I know, Dad," I told him. "I know." I had to interrupt because I did know — I had to agree with him, the place looked awful, sand everywhere you turned — but also because I just couldn't bear to listen anymore.

"You see," he said to me, "I don't even have to speak and you understand. Mom and I just don't have that."

Sometimes, even amid all that sand, I felt like I was drowning.

It was quiet in the apartment that night. My father had gone to sleep early. My mother was reading on the couch. Occasionally, she crept by me and into the kitchen for some pretzels, closing the drawer slowly with her hip so the sound wouldn't break my concentration, waiting till she had sat back down on the couch at the other end of the apartment to take the first crunchy bite.

What is the square root of 73?

Tree is to grass as plane is to what?

If a train is traveling west at 62 miles an hour, and it has 351 miles to go . . .

I arranged my peanuts across the page, a meaningless pattern. I looked at the Shabbat candles my mother had lit earlier that evening. They had melted down to tiny white stumps; the flame bobbed and flickered. I wondered what I was doing.

And while I tried to remember my SAT tutor's theory about guess-work — did you play the odds or play it safe? — one part of my brain let go and snuck away, thinking about everything beyond the beige landscape of that apartment, about all that I might be missing.

I realized it: I needed to get out of the house. I decided to do something.

On another Friday night not long after the SATs, I told my father I had to talk to him; I told him I had some bad news. It was understood that any conversation he and I had was private; we were always looking for ways to ensure my mother wouldn't overhear us, always stopping midsentence if she happened to come within earshot. We went into my parents' bedroom, and then into their bathroom, and shut the door.

"This isn't working for me anymore," I said. I said Shabbat was just isolating me, and sitting at home wasn't making me feel especially close to God or my fellow man, and though there were plenty of Jews at my school, being the only observant person in my class was too difficult, and since I couldn't write during Shabbat I often had too much schoolwork to catch up on to be able to go out on Saturdays, and I just wanted to have the same schedule as everyone else, the same obligations, the same freedom. I didn't mention the part about needing to escape.

"I'm sorry," I kept saying. I was such a devoted girl. "I really don't want to be letting you down."

There was actually a degree of urgency to the discussion. I sort of needed my father to say, *Okay, I understand,* right there on the spot, because I had already told a boy from school that I would meet him later that night. A band he liked was playing at a club downtown. This boy wore plaid sports jackets and loud ties and funny hats, and he had a knack for making me laugh so hard it looked like I wasn't breathing, and though I was still too afraid to even think about sexual involvement, in his presence colors seemed more vivid to me, and my own body felt like a fluid thing, weightless and alive. I wanted to be there with him.

My father did say okay right there on the spot. He said I was being reasonable. He saw that it was clear I had thought long and hard about this decision, that it was a tough one for me to make. Maybe he also reflected on his own high school days, the fun he had, and wished the same for me. Maybe he thought that since I refused to play tennis — I had thrown my racquet down in frustration after missing a shot when I was thirteen and, "social sports" be damned, had not picked it up since — I needed all the help I could get.

That night, the boy and I drank wine coolers on the corner before the show started. I got a little tipsy. The spring air was full and creamy, and it seemed like something else you might drink in, and inside the club, the music was loud and the air was smoky and it felt nice to stand so close to him, the cuff of his awful plaid jacket brushing gently against my hand, the material so coarse it felt like fingernails and brought goose bumps to my skin.

I got what I wanted: the freedom to have my own adventure on a Friday night, the freedom to be far away. I took cabs, the subway, the bus across town. I went out with my friends to Chinese restaurants and ate shrimp for the first time.

But the shrimp was springy in my mouth, the taste too close to ocean itself, the texture not entirely pleasant. I wasn't sure I liked where I had brought myself, or whether I had really gotten anywhere at all. Though I had removed what I thought was the barrier between me and my friends, I still felt as though I was getting only a piece of who they really were. I had the sense that things were going on that I was not privy to, that my friends needed to edit their lives for me, could not show me their whole messy selves, because I wouldn't understand, I would disapprove. Shabbat or no Shabbat, I had so many rules governing my life. I stood rigid, inert; I did not seem to have normal impulses that might bend me every which way, toward discovery, or disaster.

I was a girl who was more concerned with what was right than what was real. A high score on my SATs was pure and beautiful, a number that would not change; it was so much more appealing than falling in love, with all its potential for danger. And I was a girl who still wouldn't put off studying until Sunday, even though I could now write all weekend long, a girl who wouldn't have smoked pot with my friends after the SATs had I been there with them, because pot made you act silly, it made you lose control. I was a girl who dragged herself to gymnastics practice, who smiled to the judges at the end of a poorly executed routine.

I often felt a vague sense of sadness, and loss. I had given up so much: a certain specialness, something that had set me apart, a way of knowing where I was in the world, an identity I had offered to myself, and to others. My Jewish friends' parents always found it both honorable and charming that I was observant; my friends themselves took a certain amount of pride in remembering all the restrictions and planning ahead for me — as though I were a disabled girl whose friendship pointed to their own generosity of spirit. "The movie doesn't start until eight o'clock, so you can make it," they would say. "There's vegetarian pizza, so you'll be able to eat something."

We no longer worried about these issues. Instead, I was right there with them, nothing exceptional, laughing and eating at a Chinese restaurant with a red carpet and a permissive bartender and menus speckled with duck sauce.

In quiet moments, there was a confusing absence inside of me, as though some central piece of my being — defective or special, I didn't know, perhaps both — had been extracted. And nothing new had replaced it. I was neither here nor there; I was in no-man's-land.

Besides, there was something too tame about the way I had gone about staking my claim, something too cautious, mature, reasoned. Though I hoped for my father's approval, it might have been better, in a way, if I hadn't gotten it without a fight. It was a blessing that complicated things, made me even more confused. Because now, wherever I went, I took him with me. With his support so generously dispensed, there was little for me to butt up against, depart from, little against which to define myself. It was like botching a flip turn in the pool when I was at camp. You wanted your feet to land flat against the wall and your legs to compress so you could then push yourself back out and away — and instead only your toes made contact, and you were floating with no momentum.

Soon after I announced my break with religion, my mother followed suit. She turned the lights on and off without making excuses; she ran the dishwasher whenever she felt like it. Saturday afternoons, she went shopping, and when the plastic bags rustled as she made her way through the apartment — broadcasting commerce, money, the workings of the secular world — she did not attempt to conceal the sound. I had paved the way for her, legitimized her own impulses. She knew my father respected me more; she needed the precedent I had set. Still, when she began disregarding the rules of Shabbat, my father was angry. He said that she was taking the easy way out, that she was breaking a promise she had made to him long ago.

It was as though she was the teenager who had rebelled, made trouble in the house, surprised and disappointed her family, fallen out of favor.

For me, it all happened too easily — so easily it didn't seem quite real, wasn't the rupture I might have needed to launch myself into a new place, a landscape scary and wonderful, with towering trees and pungent flowers and soft ground where my feet could make prints.

I should have shoved some pillows under my covers, arranged them to match my shape, and snuck out to meet that boy downtown that night: a mannequin self sleeping tight while the real me misbehaved. I should have gotten caught, gotten into trouble, had a huge confrontation with my father. The process should have been less civilized; it should have been full of screaming and accusations and tears. It should have been messier, bloodier, more painful, like birth.

Shreds

n the spring of my senior year in high school, it occurred to me
that I should be writing poetry. I was not interested in poetry,
exactly. I didn't ever read it, except when it was assigned in class,
and the last time I had actually written a poem, I was in fourth
grade. My mother still referred to that poem every so often.
"Remember that lovely poem you wrote?" she would ask me.
She brought up this poem, in which I contested, in rhyming
stanzas and shaky script, that wrinkles were not a sign of old age but a
sign of beauty, when she wanted to make a point — about my brains,
my talent, my way with words. And she thought of this poem as a present I had given her just by writing it, which, perhaps, like everything I
did, it was. "Every time I look in the mirror and get upset about my
wrinkles," she said, "I remind myself of that poem, and then I feel better. Really, I do. And to think — I mean, just think about this — you
were only nine when you wrote that!"

But now I was eighteen and I decided to take a poetry elective in
school because it seemed like something I should be doing — didn't
sensitive young people write poems? — and because writing poetry
was a trend among people I admired: the girls in my class who I was
friendly with but not quite friends with, who were different in an in-
timidating sort of way and always kept their journals with them and
wore jeans with holes in the knees and scarves, all kinds of scarves, in
their thick, long hair, as though their heads — full of glorious, dazzling
words ready to spill out onto the page — were big beautiful presents
that warranted wrapping with silky bows.

I also signed up for the class because of the teacher, who had in-
formed me, when I took English with him in the tenth grade, that I
could write. He said it with confidence, as though it were a simple fact,
one more thing he was teaching me that I might not have otherwise

been aware of, like Shakespeare's birth and death dates. He may have even used words like *talent* and *gift*. There was something about his classroom that opened me up just a little bit, so there was a crack through which I got a glimpse of glorious images and heard the rhythms that language could make, and I was no longer writing dull eight-hundred-word letters to imaginary friends but tapping into something much deeper, and writing was like reaching into a clear cold stream inside of me and grabbing hold of a shiny treasure from the bottom — a penny, a piece of glass, a quiet creature with a pearly shell.

At the end of that school year, my teacher urged me to write more, to write often, which is not something I had actually done in the intervening time, but I had not let go of his encouragement, either; it was like a small living thing curled up inside of me, eyes closed, hibernating, warming me, warmed by me. I got the feeling when I was in this teacher's classroom that he was there especially for me, that I myself was special in a new way, in a way that had nothing to do with being my parents' girl or the bundle of pressures and hopes that shaped their vision of me, and everything to do with who I really was. I had found him by myself, by writing essays and compositions that caught his attention. Through my words I had made my own connection, gained a toehold in the larger world.

I wrote my poems at night, thinking of this teacher, not in a romantic or sexual way, but as though he were a loose presence in the room, an atmosphere. I wrote my drafts in a notebook, at my yellow desk, inside the cone of light cast by the desk lamp, the only light on in the room. I turned off the overhead because it seemed to me that poetry must be written — could only be written — with this kind of dramatic lighting. But it was also the kind of lighting that gave me freedom: I was taken out of context, my little-girl bedroom disappeared in shadow behind my back, it was just me and the words and the leeway darkness offered. And even though I wrote so slowly in my notebook — one painstaking line, then the next — thinking so hard about each word, wanting it perfect from the outset, crossing out phrases I didn't like, running big heavy *X*-es through false starts I was not happy with, until finally I was ready to copy my finished poem onto a fresh sheet of loose-leaf paper and stick it into my folder, I could still, in this darkness, begin to float, just a little bit, away from everything I had been, and grope for new ground. And even though the handwriting was my own — the letters crowded together, neat and well behaved, every word a tight little coil — my hands, as I produced these lines, could look pleasingly unfamiliar, full of tendons that sparked and rippled, full of muscle I never knew I had.

It was warm out already; I kept the window in front of my desk open, and the moths flocked to the screen. I watched them flap, amazed at the meat of their bellies, how sizable as creatures they really were. I was in awe. I was a senior, I was going to college soon, I was writing poems, it was springtime, and so many things astonished me; there seemed to be life in every corner of the planet. I looked at one of the moths and thought about how I would really feel its delicate architecture collapsing between a rolled up magazine and the wall: it would have weight, a marvelous presence, I would feel the squish of its insides.

Still, amid the promise and the darkness and the magical presence of the moths, my poems told another story. They were all more or less the same: they were about barriers to communication, the unlikelihood of ever being understood, the way that words didn't really do the work they were supposed to. There was a poem about two people arguing on the subway. There was a poem about a little boy who writes his name with his boots in big capital letters in the snow, only to find, the next morning, that another snow storm has come and covered it up. There was a poem about sitting down to dinner in my house, how the television did the talking, each of us at the table a planet in the cold dark of outer space. I even wrote a poem about the moths, how insistent they were, knocking stupidly against the screen, incapable of reaching the light of my lamp, about the thump of their bodies and the beating of their wings, soaked, muffled sounds, like underwater words, unintelligible. I was not aware of the theme that ran through these poems, I had no sense of what they were really about. This is just what I came up with. It was my teacher who pointed out to me, later on, that in every one of them there is despair, there is isolation, there is the absolute failure of language.

Something always shifted in me overnight. By morning, I was no longer writing for myself, or the person I might someday become, or even for the English teacher who thought I had promise. I was back in place once again, my parents' girl. At breakfast, I read aloud what I had written.

Standing in front of them at the breakfast table, sliding my new poem out of its folder, I reminded myself that though I was excited to share my work with them now, I wouldn't be happy afterward. I'd feel drained and spent, even dirty. I gave myself pep talks: *Don't do it; just walk out the door. This is a gift you don't really want to be giving.* I knew that when I read my new poem to them, something of myself would be taken away.

But it was a compulsion I couldn't seem to control. The darkness of the night before was thrilling but also scary, like walking through fog, or a snowstorm, not knowing which way is up, all my points of reference blotted out. I got a little bit dizzy. In the fresh light of morning, I felt more clear-headed. When I peeled back the covers to climb out of bed, the fingers curling around that soft edge of sheet were mine again; I knew them.

And with those fingers I reached once again for all that was familiar, even the thing that gave me great pain: that difficult knot of connection to my parents, when I was a reflection, a compromise, the fulfillment of someone else's wish. Because it was connection, still, and because it was, after all these years, how I recognized myself.

Part of me wanted to carry my poems to school with me, tucked away in their folder in my book bag, without my parents ever hearing the words I had strung together at night. This is what it meant to be eighteen. You had things going on, projects in your head, in your heart, you had a life that was developing, all yours. But I had no idea how to protect what was mine. Keeping this to myself would have been a betrayal, a bad secret, a good-bye.

So I stood at the table and read to my parents, and my father instructed me to slow down, to enunciate, and at the end my mother said, "Oh, read it one more time."

And I read it one more time and then together they said, "Oh, that's wonderful!"

"You really are a wordsmith," my father said. "Beautiful."

"Just amazing," my mother said.

Apparently, they didn't see what my poems were really about either.

After a pause my father asked me why I chose this word instead of that word, wouldn't *dusk* sound better than *evening*, perhaps I should have said *blue jay* instead of *robin*.

I felt sick, depleted, bereft.

Maybe it was the way I had shared my poems with them, the way my words and so much else about me had in a sense been theirs all along, that gave my parents the notion that they were entitled to do what they did a few weeks before the school year ended. Maybe they couldn't bear the thought of sending me off to college, of letting go. Maybe I myself had unwittingly extended an invitation to them. In any case, this is what they did: they went into my room one day, they took the folder full of poetry from my desk, and they brought it to a conference that they had scheduled with my English teacher.

The three of them met in that very classroom, the place where I was a singular person, a student, a girl, a writer of poetry. But I was not there at the time; it was a day when I didn't have my poetry class. I was in another classroom, talking about Plato or translating the *Aeneid*, oblivious. They were doing this behind my back. I found out what had happened later on, from my teacher, and this was how my imagination filled in the scene:

The desks in his classroom were arranged in a circle. My parents slid in awkwardly; my mother banged her shin on the metal leg and joked that it had been a few years. My English teacher leaned against his own desk, arms folded across his chest, suspicious.

My father pulled the folder of poems out of his briefcase and pushed it to the edge of his desk, toward the teacher. It was the evidence.

"We're here," he said, "because we think she is so talented, but she needs so much help."

"I mean, we look at these poems, and we see she has such a way with words," my mother said, opening up the folder, flipping through the sheets of paper. "But we're just not sure she's really aware of it. I mean, do you see how gifted she is? And yet, what does she do, she sits in her room all day, she — "

"We'd like," my father said, getting to the point, "we'd like for you to encourage her to write. She seems to respect you. She'll listen to what you have to say."

"So that she's doing something with herself besides just moping around," my mother added.

They had made their case, and now they both sat back in their seats, in perfect agreement, united in what they saw as their common cause.

My brother was a worry to them still, but he was out of their reach, almost finished with college, no longer a daily and immediate source of concern. Their focus had shifted to me, alone with them in the house, struggling through adolescence.

They worked so well together, my parents did, when I was their project, when I was the thing that needed fixing.

The next day, my teacher kept me after class. He said my parents had come to talk to him. He said, "They told me this was just between us but I thought you should know, I thought I should tell you." He said he felt obligated, and he felt bad for me, too, that they would do something so invasive, and yet — he couldn't help himself here — he also thought they had a point. "Write more," he said. "Write always."

He asked me to pull out my folder, and he lay the poems out next to each other along the circle of desks, and then he studied them like a fortune-teller reading someone's cards. He paused in front of each, sometimes laying his fingers lightly upon the page. And this was when he told me what he saw: that my poems were all about the impossibility of connecting with other people, other things.

"I think you should try writing about something else," he said. "I think you should try writing about connection. Words sometimes do work, people do sometimes see each other and understand." He looked at me for a long time; he had a sad and gentle and earnest face. "Those moments," he went on, "are there, however brief. And they are powerful." And I realized when he told me this, his gray eyes leaning down at the sides, that in some way what he was talking about was us, too, the connection we had, standing next to each other in this classroom, so close I could smell the oil of his skin. I had a sense, suddenly, of what words were capable of, of what I myself was capable of, I felt it in the base of my spine. It was powerful, yes, and also a little bit dangerous.

Before I left the classroom, my teacher gave me a poem by a Russian poet that was about those moments of connection, however brief. It looked like a tenth-generation photocopy: the letters were cracked and faded, the white space speckled with mysterious marks — hairs, fingernails, tear drops.

I waited until my father got home from work that evening and then confronted my parents. It was like pressing an ON button somewhere inside of me: I started by shrieking, big heavy tears blurring my vision, turning the fluorescent light into a set of wild smears across the kitchen ceiling.

"How could you do this?" I asked them. "How could you do this behind my back? My school, my teacher, my poems . . ."

My parents were surprised by my outburst. They thought I was overreacting. I sensed them pulling back from my rage, retreating, a little put off by it.

"Look," my mother said. "Calm down. We were just doing what we thought was best for you."

"I don't see what the big deal is, Deb, honestly," my father said. "We think you're terrific; we just want you to feel that way, too. What's wrong with asking for a little assistance?"

There was so much wrong, and yet I was at a loss for how to explain it to them. The right words didn't come to me. In fact, I could hardly string two words together, and in place of coherent thoughts there was a lot of cursing, and once the *fuck yous* and the *assholes* and all that came out we were at a new level, because those are words with power too, and my parents moved from bewilderment to anger.

"Is that the way you respond," my father asked me, the veins at his temples beginning to emerge, "when people are trying to help you?"

I felt blinded, toppled. I felt the three of us being sucked into something, the world closing in on me, and there was only one thing to do, there was only one way to climb up out of this rage, to escape. I went up to my room and pulled the poems out of their folder. I stood at the landing and tore them up, first into halves, then into quarters, then into tinier and tinier pieces, and when they couldn't be torn any further I threw them over the banister, they showered down into the hallway, and my parents stood in the kitchen doorway watching the display, the scraps falling so gently to the floor, falling like snow, like confetti in a parade, like the dandruff on my mother's scalp, like cherry blossom petals, like the shreds of paper that they were, like nothing I would ever have the words for.

Eclipse

y freshman year of college, I was assigned a single in a suite, which I shared with five other young women. That is what we were trained to call ourselves — women — though really I felt much more like a girl.

It was confusing, to have been bound to my parents for so long and then released into this new landscape. I hadn't been adequately prepared. I felt frozen, blank.

I slept through my morning classes — it was so hard to get up before noon and conjugate verbs in French or listen to someone explain from the bottom of a sloping lecture hall how to calculate the distance between two stars. Besides, sleep was such a wonderful retreat; in my dreams I could be anything, or nothing.

Art history was in the afternoons; this class I could wake up for, even looked forward to. It was a survey course taught by a famous professor who was histrionic, flamboyant, an engaging lecturer in love with every painting, sculpture, and building that was projected behind him over the course of the hour. He darted back and forth at the front of the room; he slapped his long pointer hard against the screen. I could sink into one of the seats and just watch.

During one of his lectures, the professor showed us slides of a series of unfinished slave sculptures by Michelangelo. The figures were twisting, animated, and with their backs still fused to the blocks of marble from which Michelangelo had begun to chisel them, they appeared to be fighting with the material, trying to wrench themselves away. The famous professor emphasized the poignancy of their predicament: they were slaves imprisoned in stone, half-formed, struggling to emerge.

He got a little choked up talking about these sculptures. I overheard some students questioning his sincerity afterward, as we were filing out through the double doors at the back of the room, but I believed his tears were genuine. I understood them. Sitting there in the lecture hall, I could appreciate the quaver in his voice. I felt moved by the sight of the slaves too. I knew the yearning these trapped figures expressed, each one's wish to break free from his maker and become his own cohesive being, fully dimensional, kinetic, taking one step and then another, discovering the subtle curve of the planet.

Meanwhile, I watched my suitemates adjust to college life, and I was amazed at their confidence. They made friends, played their violins in the orchestra, joined intramural volleyball, tutored inner-city high school kids. All around me I heard laughter, I heard people running down the halls, I heard the thump of music from other floors. The campus seemed to be filled with movie stars: people who exuded something larger than themselves, a kind of radiance.

I reminded myself that they were all merely searching, that they were trying on faces, grabbing hold of one and putting it down and then reaching for another. I reminded myself that they were as confused as I was.

But how had they learned to reach with such lust, such enviable, wholesome greed? Who had taught them to have faith in the exploration — even if what they were grasping for ended up disappointing them, not fitting right, leading them astray?

Something interfered with this process for me, though I could not name it. I was afraid of the wrong choice, I was afraid any choice meant rupture, a split from my parents into a new self; it was a separation too painful to accomplish.

All I knew was that I was paralyzed, unable to grasp, uncertain of what I might reach for.

Here is what I reached for instead of the sweet, messy fruit of life:

- half a pound of peanut M&Ms at the on-campus candy shop, where candy was dispensed from clear plastic chutes lined up like organ pipes against the wall;
- a box of Pop Tarts at Store 24. Any flavor was okay, but they had to be frosted. Frosted Pop Tarts were moister and sweeter; they made you sick sooner, they came up more easily;

- a pint of chocolate chip ice cream from Wawa's and — last minute — a king-size Snickers bar for the walk home.

Back in my dorm room, I shut the door and laid out my goods on my desk. I was breathless, my chest braided with fear, with excitement. I could not wait. I peeled off my jacket between handfuls of M&Ms and tossed it somewhere — the bed, maybe the floor. I dug into the ice cream with a spoon I had lifted from the dining hall, I tore open the Pop Tarts and bit into them two at a time. Finishing was all I thought about, this food was all I saw, this task was all I was. During this blissful, agonizing stretch of time, my universe diminished itself to a bite that I could swallow; nothing existed beyond the curve of my spoon and the melting, glistening dune of ice cream that slid off of it onto my tongue.

It was the same intense, myopic, soothing concentration that I sometimes experienced as a small child; it was a product of that low-to-the-ground perspective, the whole world fallen away as I dug into the dirt beneath the maple tree in the backyard, looking for worms to feed the robin with the broken wing, or as I touched the impossibly soft twitching nose of the class guinea pig I got to take home for the weekend in kindergarten. I pictured it as an image of my mother's lower half, the weave of her blue jeans with the bleached-out crease running down the center as I tried to talk into her hand. And I felt it as the slow back flip my father helped me through every night when he came home from work, first thing. I would grab his hands, walk up the front of his legs, and then launch off from his thighs and turn over, landing feet first on the ground, joyous, his fingers still gripping my own.

I sat at my desk and shoveled ice cream into my mouth until my lips went numb and I could no longer close them around the spoon. My brain worked in concert with itself. I was fully myself: immersed, in sync; it was a rare event.

The purge, in part, was damage control; I would not accept all those calories, I could have gained two pounds in one night alone if I had just sat tight. In part, too, it offered physical relief; I had eaten so much that I was in great pain, my stomach seemed to have expanded in all directions — upward, even, leaning against my lungs, so that breathing was difficult. But I also had the sense that I was completing what I had begun; the purge was not only a response, but a conclusion. I could not get all of this without also giving it up.

You can see, of course, that there was much more going on here, with this kind of consumption, and the about-face that followed. I was doing other things to my body, my self, when I binged; I was rejecting more than just these calories, undoing more than what I had just done, when I purged.

You can see how this behavior brought me back to myself, and at the same time back to my parents; you can see how these two were really one and the same.

But these connections didn't occur to me just then. In fact, nothing did. I never told myself a story, gave myself an explanation. I never even asked myself why. My brain just emptied out. The continuous chew-swallow, chew-swallow lulled me into a kind of trance, like counting my breaths or saying a mantra. The repetition became a rhythm that I slipped into, gave myself over to; I lost myself inside of it. Something — an impulse, a nebulous but distinctly desperate need — simply kicked in and took over, funneling the course of my evening toward this single purpose. It was a force that operated outside of cognition, precluding words and thought, precluding, even, the need for words and thought. It just happened.

This muteness now makes a certain amount of sense. I understand that perhaps, through all of this, my body was speaking for me, picking up the slack while my lazy psyche dozed, articulating through behavior the hidden, damaged parts of me that language could not reach, could not repair, could not bring to light. I see that perhaps this wordless state is one of the gifts my binges and purges gave me, the divorce from the verbal, thinking self not only characteristic of the illness but also part of its essential appeal, the eclipsing of thought through mindless action a retreat into numbed-out relief, into silence.

One day I was sitting with my journal at the counter of a coffee shop several blocks from campus. The coffee they served there was bland and burnt, but it was a townie establishment and I liked the anonymity. There was no chance of seeing someone from my French class and wondering whether I should say hello (and then what?) or just tuck my head back into my journal and pretend not to have seen her, whether she would think I was a loser for being there alone — or whether she would even know who I was.

I was scribbling away when I noticed a guy sitting down on the stool next to me. He had stringy blond hair that just touched the collar of his army jacket and a scab the size of a raspberry right above his top lip. He swiveled toward me. The left sleeve of his jacket was empty, folded at the elbow and pinned to his chest.

"Hi," he said. His eyes were deep blue and streaked with white, the way Earth looks from outer space. They kept roaming the room; he could not focus.

"Hi," I said back to him.

"So what are you writing, anyway? Are you a writer or something?"

"No, it's just a journal," I said, closing it up.

"Yeah? I write a lot, too. Stories, you know, stuff like that. In notebooks. And I draw. My whole bedroom is covered with drawings, all the walls, covered." He made a sweeping gesture with his right arm. "I'm missing an arm," he said. "Did you notice?"

"Yeah," I said. "What happened?"

"I was drunk. I was really drunk and fucked up on some other stuff, too. It was New Year's Eve, me and my friends took the train in to New York to watch the ball drop. I fell off the platform in Grand Central Station — you know Grand Central Station, in New York? Anyway, I got electrocuted, that third rail thing is no joke. I had to get my arm amputated."

"Wow," I said. "When was this?"

"Oh, I don't know." He thought for a minute, his face clouded over. "Seven, maybe three years ago. Or seven, maybe. Wait, how old am I?" His face cleared up. "How old are you, anyway?"

"I have to go now," I said, signaling for the check.

"So maybe I'll see you next time," he said, getting up with me, leaning over. "Can I have a kiss before you leave?"

He smelled unwashed, his legs looked withered, he was a complete stranger, he was crazy. But I kissed him anyway, right on the lips — reaching out for his lost limb, his disjointed story. And then recoiling. I ran from the coffee shop, I ran for three more blocks. Panting, disgusted, I spit on the sidewalk and then wiped my mouth until it was raw. I could not make myself whole.

I started therapy. Twice a week, I walked a mile-and-a-half to see my therapist and then walked the mile-and-a-half back. I made the trek in rain, sleet, and snow, and no matter what else was going on in my life. I inhaled the garishness of my therapist's outfits, the mustard tights and dark green high-heeled pumps, her enormous crimson bifocals. The elaborate baubles on her puffy knit sweaters jutted out like buoys for me to hang onto. I listened for the way she started every sentence with "You know, Debbie . . ." like it was the refrain to a lullaby someone once sang me. My profound unhappiness occurred to me then; before, it had been so out of focus: it was simply the air I breathed, a way of being, life. The awareness was new and terrifying, and these sessions sustained me: Tuesday's session until Friday; Friday's until Tuesday. My eyes blinked, adjusting to shadows and darkness; they began to make out the shapes of despair.

And there were moments of clarity, as well, like a flash briefly illuminating every tainted, cobwebbed corner and then dying. *Flash!* I could see a salmon-colored rage beginning to shift and jerk inside of me like chunks of ice melting. *Flash!* I could see a voice scratched out in hard, dark pencil — You are not enough, you want too much. *Flash!* I could see my father watching me dive into the pool, toes pointed, perfect, the hardened calves he so admired flexed as I descended. *Flash!* I could see my mother lying in bed, could see the tug of her fingers at my shoulders as I tried to walk away. And the flash burned out, but the memory of what it had illuminated helped sketch in the picture, too. There was an entire scene, inclusive of — but much larger than — this single symptom that had sent me, scared and bewildered, to my therapist's office. My shameful secret, my bulimia.

The disorder was a great help to my parents, really. I had done the awful deed of leaving; I had abandoned them, though when they dropped me off at school at the beginning of the year, they had been hopeful, proud.

"You're gonna knock 'em dead, kiddo," my father told me. "You're gonna love it." He was beaming, happy to be on a university campus again, imagining my college career would resemble his own — the football games, the late-night zaniness, the hard work, the fun.

My mother seemed like any other mother, unpacking suitcases, sliding clothing into drawers, kissing her child one last time, and then waving as the car pulled away.

But I think they must not have known exactly what to do once they got home and the excitement of sending their daughter off to college died down. They no longer had the distraction of my presence, the challenge of fixing me, and there they were, with the wall of Churchill memorabilia, with the anniversary jewels tucked away in velvet pouches, with each other: two strangers blinking in the silence of a house that seemed suddenly a little shabby, in need of tending. The grandfather clock had stopped ticking. The bushes had gotten scraggly, withered. The columns would need to be repainted in the spring.

This is what my mother talked about when we spoke on the phone, which was not very often: the errands, the little projects. But there was no excitement in her voice. She sounded smaller to me, as though some essential life force had been sucked out of her.

The glue that had held them had disappeared; the third, essential point of the triangle had vanished. I was gone. In my mind they were so lost and overwhelmed, like two dust motes swirling aimlessly in an empty room.

On the morning of my nineteenth birthday, which fell on a Sunday that year, I was awakened in my dorm room by my father's hand on my back. It was nine-thirty.

There was no phone call to prepare me; there was not even a knock on the door. Just the hand, and then me rising slowly into consciousness, and my father singing, "Happy birthday to you." He had driven the two hours to school to surprise me.

I rolled over and sat up; I was furious.

"What were you thinking?" I yelled. "What if a *guy* had been here? What about my privacy?"

He was bewildered by my indignation; he had to keep himself from chuckling. The suggestion of another man's presence was ludicrous to him, outlandish.

Of course it was ludicrous; I was too shy to say hello to men on campus, let alone go to bed with them. And this is part of what upset me so: knowing how far I was from entanglements, alone in my room night after night with my food and my oblivion.

But he was not supposed to know this. He should have assumed that I was a being with fluid contours, that I had a life with momentum; he should have at least had that expectation, instead of reiterating the stunted, rigid shape I had grown into.

"Okay," he said. "I'm sorry." It was an apology driven by respect as opposed to remorse: he didn't really see.

After a few minutes of strained conversation, he left.

I had to rescue them, protect them from their own pain, give them what they were looking for; I had to offer them the gift of my bulimia.

I did not return to school in September. Instead, I stayed in our apartment in New York. My parents knew what was going on, yet they had chosen to give me the space I had asked for and spent all their time at the house in New Rochelle. They had skittered into an awkward combination of overbearing involvement and excessive, frightened latitude: we never seemed to get the balance right. I didn't know how to seek their help; they didn't know how to give it to me.

My father drove into the city to work every day but did not stop in to check on me, though I knew he wished he could. Sometimes my mother came into town to go shopping with me, but we were strangers to each other. She sat in the Bloomingdale's fitting room watching me try on clothing. She leaned her head against the wall, looking so tired, looking weighed down by the pile of clothes in her lap: the discards, the pieces I had yet to try on. She handed me item after item, I said no to everything. It all looked terrible, my cheeks were flushing with frustration in this tiny, overheated space. We talked about nothing, my sad, sad mother and I, both of us reflected infinitely, from so many angles, in these smudged, unflattering mirrors.

Still, I was closer to them than I might otherwise be, and I knew I was foremost in their thoughts, if not physically there with them. They were strategizing, consulting professionals, talking to each other late into the night across the dark slit between their beds. I was bringing them back together; once again, they were a unified front.

They started to see a couples therapist. A few months into the therapy, they asked me if I would join them for a session. I agreed right away; I was happy to offer my own insights about their relationship. But when we got there and seated ourselves in the therapist's comfortable leather chairs, all they could talk about was me. The triangle had been reconstructed; they were once again clear in their focus.

My life had been interrupted, my growth arrested; I was home again, my parents' girl.

I spent so much time in that sand-colored apartment, looking at the walls, the carpet, which seemed to stretch out forever.

"It soothes my nerves," my mother had always said, one hand across her chest as if to contain her violently beating heart, when I was in high school and my father and I used to complain to her about the blandness of the decor. "I find it peaceful."

Now I finally knew what she meant; I saw how sometimes we need neutral zones, spaces that take us out of the world, allow us an escape from the tumble and struggle of living, from simple progress. I understood her.

For a few months, my brother lived there, too. He was in the process of buying his own place and needed some temporary housing until the deal closed. Our apartment was small, but I managed to avoid him. He worked long hours; in his free time he trained for triathlons. And when he was there, I had my bathroom and bedroom, which were really all I needed. We caught glimpses only; we did not talk.

Maybe he didn't hear the sound of my puking, didn't wonder why the toilet flushed so much. I tried not to think about it; I was too afraid to find out.

On a family vacation a few years earlier in the Caribbean, Danny and I found ourselves talking to a woman our parents' age one night after dinner. Or, rather, we found ourselves listening, bored out of our minds. Maybe she had had too much to drink; maybe she was just naturally dull.

"Excuse me for just a minute, please, if you would," my brother said. He was in college then; he had learned to talk like a grown-up.

"Certainly," the woman said. My brother walked off and never returned, and the woman resumed, talking and talking. I had no idea how to extract myself from the conversation. I smiled at her, nodded my head; her coral lips pursed and stretched, her earrings jiggled at her jaw. I was furious at Danny for leaving.

In a broader sense, this was how I felt about him now. He went to college and never came back. He seemed to have taken his whole childhood in stride. He had just walked off, gone on to the next thing, while I was trapped, incapable of moving forward. He was a little strange — inflexible, extreme in his habits, a bit awkward socially, prone to missing the point — but he was doing all right. Look at him! He had a great job fiddling with numbers and the stock market; he had a girlfriend and activities that occupied him. He had escaped.

Interlude

Here is my dilemma.

I could end with this episode. The piece would need a conclusion, of course. Because you are wondering, Well, what happened?

And I would tell you this:

I went back to school the following year, and back to seeing my therapist twice a week. Over the next few years, my bingeing and purging slowly tapered off. And finally there was a point in the middle of my senior year of college — two weeks passed, and then a month, and then I lost count altogether — and I felt safe saying that I would not binge and purge again.

I would tell you that somehow, I took the tiniest of steps, at a pace that was hardly discernible. I made a few friends. I fell in love. My boyfriend and I visited galleries in New York together; we had sex and we held hands. I was thinking about applying to graduate school, a career as an art historian.

I wouldn't be able to explain to you how it happened. I did not orchestrate this gradual shift, had no control over the pace at which the pattern of behavior lost its muscle. Perhaps I simply grew up a little, grew out of my illness, the way I had grown out of thumb sucking and dolls, and replaced it with other things. Perhaps it had something to do with the bond my therapist and I formed, what I discovered in that space — that it is possible to become a whole and separate being, to have your shadows as well as your light; that it is okay to be human, to hate, to have desire, to want to close your fist around a dark bug, eat a star, lie down in a puddle of mud.

I would tell you that when my therapist and I said good-bye after I graduated, I said I felt ready to stand on my own two feet. I said I was hopeful. I said there was a world out there, and I wanted to be a part of it.

And in a way, it would work, to end my book with a piece about this illness. It does a nice job from a structural standpoint, creating a sort of bracket for my life with "Swallow" at the very beginning. We could then see this closing chapter as the neat culmination of everything that came before, the bulimia a beautiful if violent metaphor for the central difficulties I have illustrated, the recovery, logically speaking, a resolution of those conflicts. The girl pukes and then heals herself. She triumphs; she moves on. Curtain.

The illness lends itself to this kind of treatment. It is so flamboyant; it is such an attention-grabber; it has all the drama of a grand finale. I cannot deny its power. I will insist on keeping it in proportion, in context, but even as I do so, I feel it pushing beyond the confines of that single piece, bleeding into others, demanding so much more attention. I feel it speaking more loudly than I want it to, its noise drowning out other possibilities.

That the illness can steal the show like that is one of its sneaky functions, I think. For years it grabbed my focus and obscured other things. It made me obsess about calories, about how to arrange for the privacy necessary to indulge in another binge, about how to cover my tracks. That helped me, at one point.

But it was also a red herring. It was so brutal and painful and ugly I began to think that was all that was wrong, that if I were cured of the illness, I would be cured absolutely. And that's what you would think, too, if I ended my story right here, that once the illness abandoned me, or I outgrew it, whatever it was that happened, I'm just not sure, I would be healed, whole, ready to move on.

You would expect an explanation of some grand transformation that I would not be able to deliver. I would feel pressure to sing the praises of therapy, and to publicly thank my therapist for helping me heal. You would want to hear that I got all better.

My therapist was a wonderful woman; don't get me wrong. But it didn't exactly work out that way. There were other therapists; there were hospitals, medications, slices with a sharp knife.

If I ended the book here, I worry that you would lose sight of the bigger picture. You would be inclined to call this a book about bulimia, which it is not, although it might seem to be at times. You would be in-

ere is my dilemma.

clined to think of me as a bulimic, which I am not, though I once was, and though that person still lives within me. Our culture is so quick to seize labels, to volley diagnoses, a designation from the *Diagnostic and Statistical Manual of Mental Disorders* squeezing us into narrow slots, eliminating the complexity of who we are as creatures, eclipsing too much. We forget the sensation of our own skin, a little bit damp, in hot weather, in the furrow where our spine rests; we forget the tiny precious secrets of our past, the memory of a gray cat slinking past a narrow doorway, of a bright red bucket tipping over at the beach. We forget who we are; we forget that we were ever searching to find out. We get reduced, we retreat into diagnosis, we become shorthand for ourselves.

No.

I am larger than that; I am taller and grander and wider. My dimensions extend beyond the narrow parameters of an illness — my yearnings and ambitions and potential, as well as my struggles, my awful ruts. There is more to the story of who I am than that one episode. I will not let it take center stage.

The Narrowest Path

Joan sat crumpled but restless in the corner, her long legs folded up like an insect's, her knees bouncing quickly against the arms of her chair. Between her overalls and her black Converse hightops you could see two bits of slim leg, with the palest fuzz and the white track marks of someone who couldn't leave dry skin alone. She picked at her shoelaces and peeled back the rubber trim along the soles. This was morning check-in, the start of each day on the ward, and though the doctors had instructed all of us in the room to take a moment to just turn our thoughts inward and reflect on how we were feeling, I could not stop watching Joan.

I had been, in my regular life, a pro at just sitting and turning my thoughts inward; until I got to the ward, I had done nothing but. I sat in the car on the way to and from a job where I could hardly concentrate on the newsletters I was supposed to be editing, my mind going in slow, well-worn circles of despair. At night I sat in my Cambridge apartment looking out the window, wrapped up in a blanket, crying, not noticing what I was seeing through my tears. Three times a week I sat in my therapist's office staring at the dirty beige carpet and talking about the hopelessness I was feeling. Sometimes, on weekends, I took antihistamines so I could stop thinking and just sleep, for fourteen hours at a time, waking only to feed and walk my poor dog around the block, then stumbling back into bed. I felt as though my brain were my body's sole organ, the rest of me there only in the service of its haywire functioning, the rest of the world a dull haze.

But now there was this tiny, sealed-up universe. There was Joan, there were the other patients. There was distraction. I was actually having an okay time.

"So," said one of the doctors, after a minute or two, "how are we all feeling?" She turned to face Lucy, who was sitting on her left: a prompt.

"Like hell," Joan muttered from across the room.

"Joan," the doctor said, sounding weary already. She angled her ballpoint in Joan's direction. "We'll get to you."

But Joan couldn't wait. In a few minutes, she would ask to be excused. She was having an episode, she would say. She'd say her thoughts were racing, racing, here, there, up, down, what kind of shoes was Kim wearing, what were those earrings made of, how many people were in the room, what was that noise out in the hall, did Cynthia know she had a run in her stockings. The details were without hierarchy, they overwhelmed her, she couldn't shut them out. She'd say her head felt like it was about to explode, or implode, or crack in half like a coconut.

At first the two doctors asked her to try, as hard as she possibly could, to just sit quietly and "be" with her anxiety.

"I can't just *be* with it," she shot back impatiently. "Look, just forget it, okay?" She started picking at her shoes again and mumbling to herself as we began to make our way around the circle.

Eventually, Joan was pardoned. For the rest of the hour, I caught a glimpse of her every couple of minutes through the window in the door. She was pacing the hall furiously with Sandy, the only nurse with the energy to keep up, talking up a storm and clutching some hardcover book so tightly it looked like she might break it in two. I couldn't make out what she was saying, but I could hear the steady stream of words getting louder and then softer and then louder again, like trains going by at rush hour.

Joan was always insisting — to whoever would listen — that no one was helping her. On the contrary, she said, it was being there that had made her nuts. She could barely endure the neglect; it was no wonder she had a hard time sitting still for even five minutes. When she came two months earlier she was fine, really okay, just a little nervous. But now: a complete wreck!

It was true that she had been there the longest of any of us and didn't seem to have gotten any closer to leaving. But I didn't believe her explanation. I secretly suspected it was all an act. She wasn't manic-depressive, or plagued by imaginary demons, or even anxious; she was hungry for attention, plain and simple. I imagined that when she was in her room alone, behind a closed door and with no audience, she kicked back and acted like a normal person would, sighing as she drifted off into a hard and dreamless sleep. She took every opportunity to leave the unit — ten cigarettes a day, lunch in the cafeteria, three-hour passes in the evening — but I didn't think she really wanted out.

I certainly couldn't blame her. The truth was, I liked it there, too. I enjoyed curling up in one of the ripped vinyl armchairs and filling out my menu every morning. I took my time, because even though I almost always ended up ordering the same thing — cereal for breakfast, a baked potato with vegetables for lunch and dinner — there were still choices to consider and decisions to be made, at exactly the level I was capable of: Raisin Bran or oatmeal? Which vegetables would I be in the mood for the following day? And it didn't matter that by the time I pulled the aluminum cover off my plate the broccoli had turned the color of pea soup and you could practically spread the carrots onto a roll. I still savored every meal.

In a way, it reminded me of home, my mother's unadorned cooking, the vegetables steamed for too long night after night, served plain in a tiny blue and white bowl. And as I ate in the silence of the dining area, all of us hunkering down and focused, aluminum forks scraping porcelain, the endless tension of those dinners and my parents' grief came back to me — not as a conscious thought but as a state I settled into. I felt it all deep down in my belly, a comforting presence, agonizing but familiar.

I was first in line when vital signs were taken; I chatted pleasantly with the phlebotomist as I watched him draw my blood; I looked forward to tossing back my medication from its tiny, pleated paper cup. It was a relief to let other people make decisions, to treat me like a child who could not think for herself. I gladly turned my body over to the authorities; I was happy to surrender its chemistry.

They woke me up in the morning and gave me things to do. I wore the same pair of sweatpants day in and day out — no one cared! And just sitting in the hall at night could keep me occupied for hours: Esther coming out of her room in a bathrobe pocked with cigarette burns asking for more morphine; Sherry peeing in her bed again; Herb complaining he couldn't sleep because next door Barbara was shouting, "Dear God! Dear God!" like her life depended on it. And there was Joan: rabble rouser, ring leader. She fought the nurses at every turn; she was constantly needling the other patients, trying to encourage their insanity. She wanted more bizarre behavior, she wanted it larger. She would have been delighted to see all of us running wild-eyed through the unit, shouting about snakes wrapping themselves around our bodies, tearing our hair out, eating imaginary bugs, our thin hospital robes undone and flapping behind us.

When Elaine, apropos of nothing, croaked out a barely recognizable rendition of "I Only Have Eyes for You," crooning at the fluorescent lights above us and grabbing onto the arm of a nearby chair for balance, Joan gave out a great big whoop and clapped her palms together in joy like a cheerleader after a touchdown.

"Elaine," she said, "you're beautiful. How about another one, a little bit louder." And off Elaine went. This time: "Blue Moon."

That was the thing about the unit: someone was always singing.

My off-floor privileges were still unused; I had no desire to check out the street. They even suggested that I go home for an afternoon, but why in the world would I want to, when my life was so comfortably on hold? I hadn't even looked at my shoes since taking them off when I got there.

I longed for the days when sick girls were kept in hospitals for months, where they knit, smoked cigarettes, read novels in bay window seats, looking up from the page now and then to scan the beautiful grounds outside, their heads leaning heavily against thick leaded glass.

I was there because one night, unable to sleep, unable to stop crying, I had crawled out of bed and wandered into the kitchen, picked up a hammer that was lying on the counter — I had been hanging pictures earlier in the day, a last-ditch attempt at industry — and started cracking myself on the head with it.

I was twenty-eight years old. I had not lied to my therapist at graduation five years earlier, when I told her I was happy, hopeful, ready to move forward. But all the confidence I had then, when I was on the cusp of adulthood, about to enter into the world, had vaporized when it came time to actually strike out. I panicked; I froze; I could not go forward.

I had moved up to Cambridge with my boyfriend from college soon after graduating, but we had broken up a year later. How could the relationship not have failed, with me so depressed all the time, looking to him for everything — remedy, purpose, diversion? I was afraid to step into my own life; I stood instead on the sidelines of his. He was devoted for a long, long time; he tried hard. But I weighed him down; I trapped him.

He must have felt the way I did when I was with my mother, who had made me her singular focus, who saw my growth as a betrayal; my mother, who needed sickness in order to feel loved.

I tried one medication, then another. At worst I felt no different at all; at best my pills and I went on a honeymoon of wellness. It felt like my brain had been scrubbed clean; my thoughts were sparkly and clear. I went to the gym, I went to sleep without feeling afraid to witness the glare of the next morning's light. But the romance always ended, and I was left with my sluggish bones, my despair.

There were little spurts of enterprise, and then complete collapse. I found jobs and then quit them, or got fired; I decided to apply to graduate school and then overslept the morning of my GREs; I enrolled in a professional cooking school and then gave up at soup stocks, just before the end of the first semester.

Cooking was hard, it turned out. You had to dice quickly and eyeball your liquid measurements and dart back and forth between cutting board and stove. It required an abstract faith in gesture — in sheer busy-ness — that I lacked. I saw the bustle in the kitchen, felt the heat of the stoves, heard the sizzle of butter browning in a pan, and I thought: what for?

But I had my own gestures. For example: a razor-sharp edge making cuts into the milky white skin of my forearm at night. I used the expensive ten-inch chef's knife I had bought for cooking school. It was an impressive blade, but they were shallow incisions, nothing dangerous. The blood bloomed briefly and then froze; the bandages I applied afterward were hardly necessary. There are scars now, but they aren't really noticeable; I would have to point them out to you.

Or this: an overdose of antidepressants, which is what had gotten me to the hospital the first time, at twenty-five, in the wake of the break-up. How else could I deal with such profound rupture? I had no idea how to repair myself, how to separate and grieve and move on. Instead, I finished off a bottle of pills. It was Prozac, and you could down a hundred of them and it wouldn't kill you. I knew that. Still, as I waited for the T to come that morning, already late for work, I imagined myself getting dizzy, and toppling into the tracks.

And now this: a hammer at my skull in the middle of the night. It was comforting to have fresh, pointed reasons for my tears, instead of the usual vague misery: I was in pain, the kind of pain you could locate; my head felt like a shattered plate. The focus relieved me. That was the thing about depression; it abstracted things, abstracted you, so you had no sense of what was wrong. You knew only that everything was too difficult. You didn't want to die, exactly, but you also didn't want to go on living.

I took myself to the nearest hospital and waited all night for a bed to open up somewhere in the city; it was the middle of winter, peak season for breakdowns in the greater Boston area. The sweet but ne'er-do-well boy I had been dating found me there; he said I sounded dangerously sad on the answering machine message I had left earlier in the evening and somehow guessed my path. I cried when he showed up, this lanky, sickly boy with long, tangled hair, alcohol on his breath, and a septum still red and puffy from the piercing he had recently gotten. I realized then he understood how pain is a kind of addiction: it enters into us; we seek it out. He and I slept curled up on an exam table; through the night, I leaned in hard against the bones of his fleshless body.

At dawn I was admitted to a psychiatric unit in a crumbling hospital at the other end of town. The nurses huddled inside a locked office and observed patients wandering the dark halls from behind a narrow window of reinforced glass. They curled their lips; they seemed put upon. The floors were cold linoleum, my sheets smelled like piss, my doctor had b.o. and a bad toupee. I screamed a lot. Several times I tore the sheets off my bed and threw my mattress across the room, slammed the wooden chair into the wall, angled the soap dispenser away from the sink and pumped hard until there was a giant puddle on the floor, pearly pink and smelling like roses.

I wanted to go somewhere else, somewhere better, but they said they couldn't transfer me. Insurance, liability issues, something — I wasn't in a state to understand what they were telling me. All I knew was that I felt trapped: they would not let me go.

Not until my parents arrived. I called them the morning I got there and they took the plane up to Boston that evening. Flirting with danger and death galvanized them into action; it brought us all back together again. I had learned to conjure them in that way. My father dropped his clients, his partners' meetings, everything to come to my rescue; my mother was at his side, holding her big brown pocketbook like a shield across her middle. They appeared, just like that. And when they did they worked in unison, protecting me, keeping me safe, holding the world at bay.

My father made a call to someone at the governor's office — an old Harvard connection. My mother squared her shoulders and threatened the doctors, the nurses, the administrative staff. And then, the next day, I was taken in an ambulance to this bright hospital. Here the floors were carpeted, the nurses were kind and competent, and the linens were clean. It seemed like a miracle, my parents like gods.

But I also began to realize that they were just two lost people, and my sickness didn't have all the power I thought it had to make them strong.

While I was in the hospital, my parents stayed in my Cambridge apartment. I had left the place a mess — my dirty clothes hadn't even made it into piles, crusty dishes littered the kitchen counter, there were dust bunnies everywhere — and though it was the middle of winter, snow on the ground, they had undertaken an authentic and unsolicited spring cleaning.

When they visited me on the ward, my mother gave me updates on the day's progress.

"Well, we got to the oven this morning," she would tell me brightly. Or: "Your bathtub is as good as new!"

My apartment was, indeed, spotless when I got home a week later, after the doctors and I had concluded that I was no longer a threat to myself. But of course, the clean didn't last. I had a cat and a dog who shed a lot; I tracked salt from the streets onto the floors. It was in the nature of things to get dirty again.

So on a raw day in February, about a month after I had returned, I decided to clean up. This was a big undertaking for me: while I no longer felt like hurting myself, I couldn't say I felt like doing much of anything.

I opened the cabinet under the sink and saw a bottle of Formula 409 that my parents had bought during their stay there. It was from Barsamian's, a gourmet shop not far from me. The bottle cost $3.89.

My parents seemed so small and helpless to me — to have bought Formula 409, of all things, at the most overpriced store in Cambridge; if only the sticker had said Star Market! — and yet so unfalteringly devoted: there they were, doing the best they could, trying to fix up my apartment, trying to straighten out my life.

I stood there at the kitchen counter, scraping the bright orange sticker off the bottle, rolling the gummy glue between my fingers, thinking of all the other things they might have paid an arm and a leg for there — toilet paper, milk, cereal, whatever else they needed during that week — simply because they didn't know any better. I saw them carving out the tiniest of worlds for themselves the way people shovel snow: the narrowest path allowable, nothing beyond the bare minimum. They walked the two blocks to Barsamian's every couple of days, they wrapped themselves up against the terrible cold and took Moxie to Harvard Yard every evening, they shuttled back and forth in taxis to visit me at the hospital while my car sat unused down the block. My father had spent seven happy years at school in Cambridge and had come back to visit many times since, but being there this time around was solemn business he must not have known how to tend to.

I wondered: Was it worse for him to feel so powerless in a place where he once strode with confidence, or did he retreat into distant memories and find some bit of relief, walking through the campus with my mother and Moxie at dusk? School years notwithstanding, this little city must have still seemed like a huge and foreign place that they didn't have the strength to decipher, and their daughter's apartment, the home of a stranger.

Did my father have to crouch in the shower every morning so he wouldn't bang into the shower head? Was the apartment warm enough for my mother? Could they figure out which switches turned on the lights, and did they realize that some switches did nothing at all? Did they know where to put the trash? I pictured my parents sitting in front of the television after dinner, trying to determine which station was which and how to use the remote, and then, realizing that they were too tired to watch TV anyway, giving up and heading off to sleep.

And I imagined them late at night, crowded out to the sides of my tiny bed, as far away from each other as they could possibly get, with Moxie curled up in between them. My father actually broke the window next to the bed one night in his sleep, that's how close to the edge he was. Probably a bad dream: he was kicking the enemy clear out of town, or breaking down a door to escape a fire, leading his trapped family to safety. What did they think about when the sound of shattering glass woke them? Did they laugh together in the dark and then reach across the bed to touch each other, chapped hands locking? Or did they just lie there silently, feeling the room get colder?

"We'll get you through this," my father kept saying, every time my parents visited me in the hospital, and on the phone after I was discharged. "We're going to lick this thing, no matter what it takes."

At first I had believed him. It was so easy to be convinced by his take-charge attitude, to trust that he would find some way to fix me. But I now saw the vulnerability that lay beneath this stance, how overwhelmed he felt by the magnitude of what I was going through.

He sent me ads he had cut out from magazines for expensive light fixtures that promised to cure seasonal depression; he advised me to go to the gym more. And my mother — she kept telling me to take vitamins.

Was I feeling better yet? both of them asked me, again and again and again. Was I feeling better yet? How long would it take? When would it end?

I finally understood that I couldn't rely on them. They couldn't rescue me — not really. They were scared and confused; they had no magic.

First Snow

The day I began my new life I took everything as a sign. It was January 14, and though fourteen has been my family's lucky number for generations, the signs didn't otherwise look good. *You are*, they were telling me, *making a huge mistake.*

I was moving from Cambridge to rural Vermont with my boyfriend, who earlier in the year had received a small inheritance from a great aunt he barely remembered and decided right then exactly what he would do with the money.

"I'm going to buy a house in Vermont," Alex said. He had spent a couple of months there two winters earlier and had wanted to return ever since. "Let's move to Vermont, okay?"

"Okay," I said. "Let's move to Vermont."

Alex signed on with a real estate broker and began taking weekend trips to Vermont to look at houses during the fall. I stayed home, deliberately keeping myself in the dark, not even visiting the area or the house he eventually settled upon. After living a fearful life for so long, I wanted to feel, for once, what it was like simply to jump. I was ripe for an adventure.

Of course, there is no such thing as a new life. There is only the person I am. Still, in the spirit of adventure, I chose to frame the day like that anyway. It was monumental enough: at the very least, I was about to remove myself from everything I had known and set up camp in an alien culture: a place where there were cows and dirt roads and who knew what else, a place my parents had never even visited. But the event was really only a shorthand, a dramatic device in the story of who I was, the most obvious outward sign of a process that had been going on for a long while, imperceptibly.

I had been living in Cambridge for seven years and begun to feel stuck there. It seemed I was operating within a set of cautious parameters that I might have finally outgrown, subscribing to a definition of myself that perhaps no longer applied: hopeless slacker, prone to funks and hospital stays, supported still by doting parents.

Among other things, they were footing the bill for my therapy — had paid for my thrice-weekly sessions for nearly six years. Perhaps it was because they were buying that they felt they were owed a piece of the process. Perhaps — and you can see by now (can't you?) why I might suspect this — they would have expected the privilege of getting involved no matter what.

"Let me in on what goes on there a little bit," my father often said. "Tell me how it works, tell me what you two talk about." My mother took a sneakier route, calling Dr. Hanson on the phone directly, asking her how I was doing, urging her to discuss the benefits of vitamin D with me in session. Dr. Hanson and I both refused to let them interfere, but when they tried I had the same awful feeling as always — I felt trapped, suffocated; I felt a rage so big it scared me.

They wanted to know how Dr. Hanson was helping me, if she was helping me at all. They questioned her competence. In their defense, I have to say it must have been hard to trust her; after all, I had found my way into the hospital twice in her care. But their suspicion meant they were distrustful of me too: they felt they knew better. They allowed me to see her anyway, but that was just the thing — they were directing the action.

So the very act of trying to recover, break away, become a being that was both separate and whole — which is really what my work in those sessions boiled down to — had my parents built right into it. They shaped the process, they had so much say. And I wondered: would we be forever intertwined?

Still, something about therapy worked, though I couldn't have explained to my parents what was happening if I had wanted to. Nor can I now; the hundreds of hours I spent with Dr. Hanson seem, for the most part, to have vaporized. I am left with physical details: the stained beige carpet; the peeling paint, skin-colored; the teddy bears and children's board games jammed into the bookshelves; a puppet folded over beneath the couch. She saw a lot of children in her office; sometimes I thought about them struggling there — seizing bright red blocks, piling them up, throwing them, their hands communicating what language could not — and I wanted to cry.

What I remember most is the silences between us, Dr. Hanson carefully watching me. Her eyes were beautiful, big and deep brown like my mother's, but they were rounder, more open, and when my gaze met hers, they were full of compassion, and behind that, there was a certain stillness. They rested gently on me. Maybe that's a large part of what I needed: a place where I could sit quietly and struggle to figure out what I was feeling, in the presence of a woman who would not overwhelm me, a woman who could help me pull away, who could herself let go, who would not see my freedom as abandonment.

There were times when I lashed out at Dr. Hanson, when my faith in her — in us — wavered, and times when I felt so full of despair I could not lift my head to speak. But those moments helped. I have come to believe what she told me so often back then, that rupture is not so bad in and of itself, it is what follows that really counts: how expertly you are able to sew up the tear. You can practice your stitching, it can be learned, and I got better at it in her office, each time she and I negotiated a return to each other, to ourselves, to the process. All those moments showed me something about myself and the world. They showed me I didn't need illness to connect, I didn't need to slice my forearms to find myself. They showed me the right kind of love wouldn't smother me, shut me down; it would open me up. These lessons were entering my bones, my blood.

I was thirty years old. I had a partner, I had begun to write in earnest. A maturity had settled in, an adjustment of expectations. I was not feeling fixed or cured, which is how I regarded myself when I graduated from college. I was just feeling better, and for right then, that was enough. I had faith that I would keep going, keep changing, and though it was the kind of change you don't really notice, I believed the million little successes I experienced, so trivial they didn't even register, were adding up to something — Dr. Hanson told me this too — the way flakes fall one after the other, until the ground is finally covered with the season's first snow.

It was snowing in Cambridge the morning of my move, five degrees. A mix of rain and snow the night before and then a steep drop in temperature had turned the whole Boston area into a maze of icy, treacherous roads. When the radio woke me up with a warning — the deejay urging listeners not to drive unless they absolutely had to, her voice sounding ominous in my almost empty room — I took her message a little personally: *You'd better just stay put, young lady.*

But I went. Alex was already at the house settling in, and I was on my own on the drive up. The sky was metallic and heavy. *It should be sunny today,* I thought. *The sky should be the brightest, most auspicious blue.* Instead, there were intermittent flurries and strong winds. Eddies of snow whirled around the black tar; the air was too cold to bind the flakes to the ground. Somewhere into my second hour, the traffic thinned out significantly. The landscape became mountainous; the jagged forms seemed to be alive, snaking slowly alongside the highway, stopping only temporarily to observe my passage. My shoulders were tight; I developed a kink in my neck that I couldn't undo.

It felt like I was driving to the end of the world.

Then, at dusk, I got there.

For a few moments I was fine. The house came into full view as I pulled up the ess-curve driveway and I recognized it; it looked exactly as it did in the picture I had seen, no better or worse.

But once I got indoors, my eyes became roving cameras, wild and impatient. When Alex leaned down to kiss me in the doorway, I could not focus on his face. I was already looking past the curve of his head, catching sight of the elaborate cobwebs that hung in high corners, sagging at the center from their own weight.

It was gloomy inside; the wood paneling soaked up most of the available light, throwing back dingy yellow circles that seemed more like shadow than illumination. The mottled carpet suggested something vague but unpleasant, particles of old and unnameable sin clinging to the gray-brown pile.

Alex had purchased the house as is, and everywhere I turned there were things I didn't recognize, things that once belonged to other people: a broken laundry basket filled with wire hangers, wine glasses veined with cracks and covered in a thin film of dust. In one of the kitchen drawers I found dull knives and Band-aids; when I closed the drawer the front panel snapped off. There was an old, dried-out bar of soap in the shower, and a big bear skin hanging at an angle on one of the living room walls.

The house was, in the language of real estate sales, a "fixer-upper" with "lots of potential," "a great first home." In other words, it was falling apart. The mudroom had begun to break away from the main structure; on the way in with my second load of luggage, I noticed a small hill of snow in one corner — accumulation direct from the skies above. The joists supporting the bedroom floor upstairs had slipped out of place. The dining room, a later addition, was propped up on a few alarmingly slender posts, which had begun to buckle; everything in the room leaned ever so slightly south.

After Alex and I unloaded the car, we lay down together on the built-in daybed in the living room. The foam cushion, which poked through the teal corduroy cover at either end, was beginning to disintegrate. I stared up at the paneling, seeing faces in the knots in the wood: a baboon, a baby seal, a wolf.

"So what do you think?" Alex asked. "Are you okay?"

The truth was I didn't feel safe there, yet I couldn't figure out why. I was afraid of the house; the woods behind it terrified me. But I was not scared that the floor would cave in on me, or worried that an axe murderer was lurking in the pines. The fear was less focused than that — bigger, but also more vague. "I don't know," I told him. "Maybe I'm just homesick. But maybe" — I was sitting upright now — "maybe this whole thing was just a terrible idea."

"You'll get used to it," he said, his hand resting on my belly. "I really think you will."

"I need a drink of water," I said, and climbed over him and headed into the kitchen.

"Um, you might want to be careful with that," Alex called after me.

"What do you mean?" I asked. But as the water started to fill the glass I saw exactly what he meant. The smell of sulfur and rust was overwhelming. I had to hold my nose in order to drink.

Over dinner at a chilly and brightly lit Mexican joint, Alex told me about the skiing he had done, the construction job he had already found in the paper. He seemed different, even after only a couple of days there. He was wearing clothing I had not yet seen him in: wool pants, union jack underwear. His hair was tousled; he had started to grow a goatee. His face looked rougher but also more radiant. His cheeks shone. I reached across the table to touch them, wanting to get to know this new man.

I felt slightly nauseated at bedtime and then threw up all night long into a huge aluminum frying pan that I found in one of the cupboards.

Alex carefully emptied the pan out and set it back down again by my head.

For three days, a high fever kept me shivering in front of the fire beneath two blankets and a sleeping bag. I slept on the daybed; a new snowstorm in Boston had delayed the movers, so none of my furniture had arrived. At night, Alex slept in a sleeping bag on the floor next to me. I was unable to stomach any food, I drifted in and out of sleep. Whenever I opened my eyes I saw the bear stretched across the wall, its mouth open, its lacquered black nose gleaming in the firelight.

My parents had bought me the Cambridge apartment Alex and I lived in, and when it sold I felt a kind of lifting, a release. I had been entangled, my limbs crumpled by smothering love; my muscles had atrophied. Suddenly it seemed there was a little room for me to stretch, to fill my lungs fully with air. I was beginning to discover my true dimensions. I was excited.

But lying on that daybed, I wanted, the next time I opened my eyes, to see the brightness of my old bedroom again, the white walls, the honey-colored floors. It was an airy place; in my memory now, it loomed as heavenly. I pictured it floating, detached from the rest of the building, disconnected from the other apartments whose residents slipped unkind notes about our dogs under the front door and gave us disapproving looks in the hallway. I thought of breezes, and curtains billowing around the three wide windows, though in all my time there I had never actually gotten around to dressing them.

Maybe that's where I really belong, I thought, *in the cradle my parents provided. Maybe I'm just not cut out for this life in the woods, this life beyond their reach.* My illness felt like a failure of will, my body caving in to its own frailty.

My fever broke the day the movers were scheduled to arrive. The sky was a silky blue, the sun was brilliant. The cold spell had given way to warmer temperatures. I was filled with optimism; suddenly it seemed that my discomfort could be relieved by nothing more complicated than the sight of a bright yellow Penske truck lurching up the driveway.

But the arrival of my furniture helped only somewhat. Because while I was surrounded by objects I had known and loved, their presence also served to highlight the strangeness of the setting in which I now found them. The matching cherry veneer bookcases, which had looked so elegant side by side behind the dining room table in my Cambridge apartment, now challenged each other from opposite walls of a narrow hallway like two football players ready to butt heads. My beloved sofa sat awkwardly against the wall. Its cushions seemed stiffer, its shape a little boxier; it looked like a nervous guest, tight-lipped and tense. My belongings seemed as unnatural as I felt there, a cardboard cutout superimposed onto a photo of snowy Vermont. We were in this place, but not yet of it.

My plants, some of which I had had for several years, all froze on the moving truck during the three-day holdover in Boston. I asked the movers to bring them inside anyway. Though all the leaves hung limply, the plants were still full and green, and they gave the impression that a warm night in front of the fire would bring them right back to life. They sat indoors for a couple of days, lined up against the wall, looking pathetic, like a bunch of bony girls with wet hair. Finally I gave up and tossed them into the woods.

It took a few days for us to clean the house and eliminate all the odds and ends that the owners had left behind. There were already leftovers piled up below the house — boots and fishing gear and broken chairs and an early edition computer — so we decided we would just add to the collection. We pulled the drapes off the windows; they still reeked from years of cigarette smoke, and the pink flowers blooming against the navy background looked ridiculous, like cancerous growths, too lush for this rustic setting. We picked up crumpled cigarette packs, though sometimes the dogs got to those first, rooting them out of corners and then tearing them into red and white confetti. We put the drapes, the dull, greasy knives, the broken microwave, the dusty, cracked wine glasses, the beer bottles, all of it into boxes and then heaved them under the house: the discards of other lives heaped up in freezing piles.

There was something satisfying about this hard labor, all the packing and tossing, the little spaces it opened up, and I threw myself into it. I didn't like the way so much of the past remained; I was trying to banish the ghosts — not only the couple who built the house, but also their two kids, who grew up there, whose names and heights were scratched into the door jamb in the back bedroom: Jake and Leanne neck and neck in the eighties, then Jake sprouting past his sister by

1995. There was other evidence of their presence. Just behind the house, the remnants of a tree fort hung between a cluster of three trees, lattice work and broken spirals stretching from trunk to trunk like an enormous spider web. To the right of the tree fort was a rusted swing set. The wall outside the bedroom was covered in graffiti — messages to Leanne written in the clear and bubbly handwriting of teenage girls. Glow-in-the-dark stars, affixed at regular intervals, decorated the ceiling of the upstairs bedroom. They lit up in the palest green for a minute or two after we turned out the bedside lamp at night.

The couple eventually divorced. The man moved to Maine; the woman moved with the kids into a house just down the road. They had been gone for a few years, renting the house out to other tenants. But I felt them still.

I needed to get rid of them. I needed to know that you could scrub and toss and start out fresh. I needed to know that you could create a space without history, that family did not have to haunt you.

I was angry at Alex for bringing me to this place, for not taking better care of me. But I didn't say anything, because I was equally angry at myself for needing that kind of care.

But the expectation was there. I had had so little experience at independence, at getting my bearings in new terrain, navigating bumps in the road. How many times had my mother gripped my hand too tightly on the playground? How often had my father pointed out the pebbles in my path? And if I was not allowed to fall — all control lost for a dizzying moment, gravity dissolved, limbs everywhere — I was also denied the chance to reorder the world once again, setting things straight with my own body, my own power, and then standing — bleeding, perhaps, but stronger. I learned to rely on my parents; I learned to need them. And there they were again when I was in my twenties, stepping right in to rescue me — to pay the hospital bills, to support me when whatever work I could find began to feel like a crushing weight and I had to find ways to get fired, to buy me a beautiful apartment when I struggled to wake up each morning. At least there would be sunny rooms to wander, the thinking went, when I finally got out of bed. At least that much would be made easier for me. My struggles were real and overwhelming, but there was always money, and I was used to being saved.

Alex, on the other hand, had no bright, freshly painted walls to wake up to when crisis came. His landlady during college is forever sanctified in his mind, because she did not judge when she heard him crying loudly through the night in a tiny bedroom upstairs, and because she never made him pay for the broken doorjambs and dented walls. How much further Alex seemed to have gotten because he had dragged himself alone out of the scariest muck.

Could I blame him because I had grown accustomed to a certain level of comfort, because what had made things easier for me earlier on was making things harder for me now?

Alex, whose father was a navy pilot, had moved six times by the time he started high school; he lived in faraway places like the Philippines and Japan. The only constant was the daily terror inside the walls — alcoholic parents battling each other and their three children. Moving was all he knew, and it became his own way of life, too. To him, anywhere could feel like home without much fuss.

When he moved in with me back in Cambridge, the whole process took an hour. He dropped a collection of duffels and backpacks and fifty-gallon trash bags onto the living room floor and then unpacked them in a matter of minutes, jamming his clothes, as they emerged, into a couple of utility shelves in the laundry room — boxer shorts next to bike shorts, dress shirts next to ski pants. I leaned against the wall and watched him, marveling at how streamlined he was, how efficiently he operated. He had been living in his sister's damp basement for a few months, and as he unpacked, the room took on the wet, green smell of mildew. It filled me up like mossy breath, life persisting quietly in darkness.

Next, he set a few sun-bleached, water-damaged photographs of family members on an empty ledge in the study. Then he said, "Let's go rent a movie." That was that.

And yet I could tell that what looked smooth and efficient to me felt ragged to Alex. He was tired of his transience; he wanted a sense of place that extended beyond the dimensions of his backpack. After all, he had his heart set on this ramshackle house — not because he thought it was a beautiful structure or a savvy investment but because it was something that might be his.

He was taking his first stab at being settled — in a house whose angles were not quite right, whose bathroom sink was held up by a couple of lumberyard scraps. The poignancy of his effort softened the edges of my frustration. We had both arrived in our present bodies strangely: I had not grown up, he had not been a child.

Still, my urgency about the house isolated me. Alex never had money; he was an expert at making do. He had lived out of his truck before, had slept in only a sleeping bag for months at a time. Before moving to the East Coast, he worked in a wilderness therapy program, where every other week, year-round, he spent eight days in the Utah desert with a bunch of drug-addicted teenagers who threw rocks when they were angry, who ran away in the middle of the night, who had not known love. Our shower was so small you couldn't bend over without banging your head into the wall, but while I had trouble shaving my legs, he didn't notice how tiny the stall was. He could choose his battles well. His showers lasted thirty seconds anyway.

This was our first official home together, but the house became a space between us — pointing to essential differences in attitude and history, a failure to match wish with capability. There was a sense of competition, suddenly, or at the very least the feeling that a challenge had been obliquely extended: Would I measure up? Would I do okay here? Happiness loomed large and out of reach; it became a prize I wanted to win. My adaptability became the measure of my worth. *See, Alex*, I wanted to tell him proudly, pointing a smooth leg in his direction, beads of water still running down my body. *I have learned a different way to shave my legs.*

When it rained, we heard it. The drops of water drilled against the roof, sounding metallic and heavy.

One rainy night, I dreamed there was a leak in the hallway, right by the front door. The water poured in; there was already a huge puddle inside the area rug by the time I noticed. I put a green watering can on the floor, but it filled up in a matter of seconds. Then I realized there were holes all over that part of the ceiling. Water poured in as though it was raining inside; no collection of pots and trays and watering cans would contain it.

In the dream a door opened behind the row of coats in the hall closet, and I stepped through, into a suite of rooms. They were gray and slightly misty; the walls looked like wet clay. A woman wearing a red kerchief and a long pleated skirt passed me silently. She was the landlady; she rented out these rooms.

I was amazed. I couldn't wait to tell Alex that there was a whole section of the house we never even knew about. We could rent the rooms to make some extra money, we could turn them into more living space for us. Separate studies, a second bathroom, a guest room for friends who wanted to retreat to the country. There were so many possibilities, so many ways to inhabit our home, so many chambers that had yet to be discovered.

I headed back toward the main part of the house to find Alex, but stopped just inside the closet. I looked back. The kerchiefed woman passed again. Her skirt reached to the floor, concealing her feet, so she seemed to be floating by. I looked the other way; the rain was still streaming into the hall.

I stood in the doorway, straddling the threshold between hope and despair.

It didn't take that long for me to get my bearings, really; I surprised myself. The acclimation felt purely physical at first, a slow erosion of foreignness that happened at its own pace and could not have been orchestrated.

Coming home from the supermarket one evening a few weeks after arriving there, for example, I realized that I was not counting driveways or reading the numbers on the mailboxes; I was thinking about what to make for dinner. At a certain point my brain decided it was safe to let go of the route home and make room for other things: *Shit! Are we out of onions? Will it take too long to defrost the chicken?* My body remembered when to stop and when to turn.

Knowing where home was, I allowed myself to roam, trying to establish a connection with the outside world. I introduced myself at the post office; I found the café that served the best coffee in town; I took up cross-country skiing; I sent my resume and clips all over the place. Suddenly an opportunist, I tried to meet people because you never knew which casual encounter might lead to something.

This kind of industry was new to me. I had always been one to find excuses, to allow caution and fear to render me inert. But now fear was my great motivator: I was afraid of always feeling the way I felt in those first few weeks, and I committed to fighting that fate. I was lonely, lost, unsure how to structure my day, while Alex worked eight to four-thirty, building a beautiful barn with a shiny tin roof a couple of towns away in the cold. At quitting time he had something new and sturdy to look at. If I slowed down, I had only the cobwebs I couldn't reach to ponder.

In a sense, the terrible condition of the house proved to be a blessing in disguise, nudging me along in my pursuit of a life. My Cambridge apartment trapped me within its walls. The comfortable interior — bright, filled with gleaming new appliances — served as a climate-controlled environment in which to incubate and coddle my natural reserve.

This house, on the other hand, was no cozy nest; its inhospitability pushed me out the door. The temperature inside was a presence that actually asserted itself. Sometimes I was forced to wear gloves when I typed. The darkness was oppressive; the rooms were cavelike, even in the middle of a sunny day. It was much brighter outside, and much warmer in the car once the heat got working. For relief, I would get into the car and just go. But I discovered that driving down winding country roads — running errands, observing the mountainous, snow-covered landscape, finding shortcuts, waving to my neighbors — made me not only warm but happy. I had begun to reshape my conception of home not as a resting place but as a point of departure.

I didn't tell my parents about any of this. These were my adventures, this was my turf. Knowing they had never driven down those roads made it easier for me to explore them myself. It made it easier for me to try figure out who I was.

It was a policy of preservation, one I had initiated much earlier, but as time passed, I held more strongly to it. I could not share with them what I was going through — my failures, even my successes. Doing so would have compromised the integrity of these experiences, it would have compromised the person I was as I went through them. When I got my first acceptance from a literary journal that winter, I held my tongue. It was Alex who broke the news to them.

But a part of me was glad he did it, a part of me wanted them to know. There was a tug so deep inside of me.

And despite the huge distance, all the privacy, the guarded conversations on the phone, I carried my parents with me anyway. Sometimes, on the ski trails, I felt them watching me. Though neither of them knew how to ski, I heard them critiquing my form, I heard them marveling at how quickly I had picked up the sport. I saw my father grinning broadly, so proud; I saw my mother shivering in the cold.

I almost always fell after that.

One Saturday night, Alex and I went to a fiftieth anniversary party for the local ski resort. The crowd was eccentric, and though the invitation said formal attire, I saw everything from evening gowns to stretch pants and snow boots, from tuxedos to knickers and argyle socks.

There was a swing band playing, and when Alex tilted his head toward the dance floor and then reached for my hand, I gave it to him without resistance. Too concerned about looking foolish, unwilling to give up caring, I had always been someone who did not dance. It was one of the first things Alex found out about me.

"Do you like to dance?" he asked me one day soon after we met. We were sitting on a park bench watching our dogs tussle. It was our dogs who had introduced us.

"I don't dance," I told him, "unless I'm really drunk."

"Well," he said, "I don't want you getting drunk on our first date." I was so charmed by the combination of kindness and daring that I did not notice his disappointment.

What made him bother asking me that night? Maybe he had never given up hoping that I would someday happily follow him onto a crowded dance floor. Or maybe he just had a hunch that this time around, things would be different. Maybe he knew before I did that this move had offered me a certain freedom, a fresh edge of possibility as arresting as the clear, ice-cold Vermont air. I had been released somewhat from the burden of past performance, the constraints of expectation. If moving did not turn me into a whole new person, it at least allowed undiscovered parts of me to rise up to the surface and shine.

I danced that night without my shadow. I twirled and spun.

Splinter

was doing fine. For a while, life had been okay, a steady ride, one day to the next. I woke up at a decent hour in the morning and went to bed at a reasonable time of night and in between I got stuff done without thinking too hard or being bothered too much by doubt, dread, despair. These were things I had come to rely on. I had had my hospitalizations, my terrible mix of medications, my years of therapy. But it had been just long enough. I was nudging my way into complacency, a sense of safety, a kind of arrogance.

Then one day, I woke up and I was not myself. I was an old self reborn, or a different self who surfaced and took over. It happened every so often. Just like that. I would be given no warning signs. There would be no slow descent, no time to prepare. Suddenly, everything made me cry, my legs wouldn't move, I couldn't get work done, I forgot the point of showering, it was hard to open a jar of jelly. Suddenly.

It was a glorious spring morning, sunny and dry and breezy, and I was sitting on the couch, staring out the window, an open book in my lap. I could not concentrate enough to follow the thread of even two sentences. My head hung to one side, impossibly heavy, my hand rested on the page like some stupid, ugly creature — a frog on a lily pad. I had no idea know how long I had been there. Morning, and I had already ground to a halt. The dogs swarmed around and nosed me — my arms, my neck — curious, cautious, as though I were a dead animal they had discovered in the woods. I felt dead to myself.

How is it that I could feel dead? Because part of me — some glowing piece, an essential ember — separated and watched what was happening, did not experience death exactly but recognized the burden of dead weight. The dreadful pull.

Later, I joined Alex in the yard. The two of us had planned to build a composter that day, but in light of my diminished capacity, he assumed responsibility for the project himself and suggested, for me, a more manageable task: Could I please create a stencil of his initials, *AK*, using cardboard and a utility knife, and then, with this can of purple spray paint, mark his tools with those initials so that there was no confusion at the construction site where he would be starting work on Monday?

While he cut wood and banged nails, I leaned over the sawhorse and drew thin lines with a black pen and then connected them into block letters. I was upset because the *K* came out bigger than the *A* but I started slicing anyway, keeping my focus narrow: one black line, the next. By the time I paused to check my work, I had already made an irreparable error. I should have kept the little triangle inside the top of the *A* solid, attaching it with arms to the outside lines. Instead, I gouged it out. Now the *A* looked like a pyramid on stumps, hardly recognizable.

I shoved the piece of cardboard across the sawhorse toward Alex. He shrugged his shoulders. "Keep going," he said. "It's close enough." I could not believe his kindness, his perfect equanimity. It was miraculous, unreal. It unsettled me, to be given something so precious and heavy as his love.

I wanted to quit right then and go take a nap, but I decided to continue the job. I owed him at least that much. But then the knife slipped and I sliced across the entire bottom of the *K*, not only the ends of the two legs but also the space in between. I found that I was crying. There was no build-up: I started by bawling. I felt as though it was taking all my strength not to collapse beneath my own enormous weight. Even my tears seemed leaden, ponderous beads that dropped to the ground and dented the soil. Alex put down the four-by-four he was about to cut and wrapped himself around me. He braced me while I shook, he ran a gloved hand across my head. His smell — sawdust and sun — comforted me. I pulled away, finally, and turned back to the stencil.

"It's fine," he told me. "Really, it'll be fine. Look, it doesn't matter; it's just a symbol anyway."

And then, as if to demonstrate his faith in my work — his faith in me — he spray painted his initials onto the table saw.

"See?" he said. "It's perfect." But to me it was all wrong, useless hieroglyphics, a half-formed, foggy thought. He had sprayed too heavily, and the paint bled past the edges, creeping out in all directions. He didn't seem to notice. He pointed to the other tools that needed stenciling and then turned again to his work. I watched him. He was industrious, his tool belt stocked with nails and screws and measuring devices. Yellow dust flew off the blade of his table saw. I could feel my eyes swivel in their sockets as I tracked his movements. Otherwise, I was frozen in place, holding the spray paint in my right hand like a torch. I knew what I was supposed to be doing. I had made sense of his words, I understood the task I had been assigned. It was my body that would not perform. I was simply stuck. The sun struck my back.

I was amazed at how long I could stand there doing nothing; the simple act of holding myself upright and watching engaged me fully. I noticed that I felt, truly, *inside* of my body; it was not a part of who I was but a casing for a shrunken, cowering self. I felt as though I were peering out at the world through slits in a Halloween costume. My skin seemed loose, crinkly, inauthentic.

After a time, Alex paused again from his work and suggested I begin to demolish the rotting deck so that over the weekend the two of us would be ready to start building a new one: it was our next project for the house. I imagined he suggested this work because he thought there would be some therapy there, and it didn't seem like such a bad idea to me, either: smashing up the wood with a sledgehammer, tearing out rusty nails with the hammer and cat's paw just as he had taught me the other day. Mindless, forceful movements; swing and hack.

I am an athletic person, my body is usually strong, but when I got out there I found that I could hardly lift the sledgehammer, and when I swung it down it fell with no force beyond its own weight. The deck did not come apart. Every rusty nail stopped me dead. I stared at my tools: cat's paw, hammer, sledgehammer. I didn't know which one to use, could not figure out how to rip off this jagged plank of wood, tear out that metal bracing. The notion of leverage confounded me.

How stupid I had become.

Hearing no banging or creaking or toppling, Alex came over from behind the house to check on me. He demonstrated some demolition techniques. I was stunned by his efficiency, the force of his swing, the way his tugs accomplished things.

"Don't take any crap from this deck," he told me. "Use your muscle."

But when he left, the sledgehammer was as heavy as ever, and all I could do was lie down on the deck. The soft wood sagged beneath me.

I'll lie here until the sun hits that pine tree, I thought. And then, *Until it reaches that branch*. And then, *Until it sinks into the hills*. Finally, I got up and made my way back to Alex's work area. I noticed that all of his tools were now stenciled. They lay in clusters on the ground looking diseased, the initials swollen and purple, like pockmarks.

He had made great progress with the composter. One side was already rooted into the ground: a square of hemlock, rough-sawn and golden, framing a taut stretch of hardware cloth. He took the level and set it on top. The air bubble slid way over to the right.

"Shit," he said.

Eventually, this would pass, as any storm does. I knew it would: enough storms had come and gone already. I could not see beyond the rumbling skies, but I could at least remember that there was a color blue, that there were times when I was weightless. I could listen to Alex when he told me that this had happened before, and that just the other day I laughed so hard he thought I had stopped breathing. I could believe him.

A couple of days later, I woke up refreshed. The world came into better focus, colors seemed more acute. Once again, I rode the sharp edges of experience. A hummingbird zipped past my window that morning, following a ragged, indecipherable course. It was the first hummingbird I had ever seen in my life. I was overcome with delight. To step into wellness again, it was a gift, a lesson: I was learning humility, and vigilance. I was learning not to take that hummingbird's frantic, blurry flight for granted. I was learning to hoard my joy.

I had no idea why these moods came upon me, or why they left. But I began not to worry about that too much. I put less stock in the downswings; they no longer terrified me. I understood that sometimes I felt lost, disconnected, that sometimes I was a splintered being, a broken thing. I understood also that I would always move toward wholeness again. The world was filled with tools for tearing and hacking, but inside there were more delicate instruments at work, forging and sanding and soldering, piecing me back together.

In Which Our Heroine Shares
Something Important about Life

bby and I were at the reservoir, standing at opposite ends of a concrete beam that stretched from one bank to the other. That's what everyone called this place, the reservoir, though in reality it was just a short stream that ran between two streets in the middle of our suburban neighborhood, my house a couple of blocks away, Abby's house a couple of blocks away in the opposite direction. It had high banks that were too steep to walk down; you had to crawl to the water, crablike, and there were big smooth rocks to play on at the bottom, and fat gray rats that occasionally scurried past, the mud training their fur into pointy chunks. My mother pronounced it *resevwah*. She said, "You kids going to the *resevwah* this afternoon?" She didn't know about the rats.

Lately Abby and I had been playing down there a lot. We were eight years old and up for adventure, but not really looking for trouble. This was our piece of wilderness, laced with a hint of danger, but bracketed by all that was safe. We felt like we were roughing it there, splashing where rats had been, getting ourselves dirty, climbing and leaping and leaving deep footprints in the muck. Sometimes we came across an empty beer can wedged in between some rocks, and I knew that teenagers were responsible — it's what my mother said, shaking her head, "Teenagers," whenever we saw property defaced or trash on the ground, the pronouncement part accusation, part lament — and I thought of bad things happening there at night, boys with greasy hair leaning back on their elbows, cackling at the moon. "Teenagers," I said to Abby, shaking my head. One of us would scoop up the beer can to throw in the garbage when we left, and we both grew sad thinking of the Indian in the TV commercial with the big tear sliding into the grooves in his cheek. Down at the bottom, where the water flowed, our perspective was eclipsed by the steep banks. Abby and I couldn't see the houses that lined the smooth paved roads on either side of us, and it was easy to believe the whole planet was dark and uncivilized, a place of ruin and rot.

But it was also easy to climb up the banks, brush ourselves off, and go back to Abby's to watch Merv Griffin and eat Velveeta with crackers. We couldn't see those houses, and yet we knew they were there: neat shutters, flagstone walks, front doors with shiny brass knockers. We knew where we were in the world.

Abby and I decided to test our balance by walking back and forth along this concrete beam, twenty feet above the water. The beam was wide enough for us to stand with our feet together but not much wider than that. We walked toward each other, gave high fives in the middle, turned and walked back.

"That was too easy," I said. "Let's try running." And that turned out to be too easy also. We decided to skip; then we decided to hop.

"Now," I said, "let's try hopping with our eyes closed."

"You go first," Abby said.

I closed my eyes and hopped along the beam, little hops at first, the sole of my sneaker barely leaving the concrete, my arms out to the sides, big wobbly pauses in between. *Don't fall*, I told myself with each hop. *Don't fall, don't fall, don't fall.* After several baby hops I stopped thinking about falling and took bolder hops, hops with a little more lift, a little more speed, then bolder hops still. It felt so strange to be jumping away from this hard, rough surface, straight into space, with my eyes closed, my lids fluttering and squeezing shut, a half-smile on my face, so strange to be launching myself against gravity, pushing up, my body frozen for a zillionth of a second at the height of my jump, and then pulled downward, with no sense of where I was except through the feel of my right foot hitting concrete, landing solidly, each hop a dive upward, upward — and then my foot missed and I was falling onto the bank of the stream.

I sank through space so fast there was no time to understand what was happening. Only afterward, only in retrospect, could I form an impression: the side of my sneaker scraping the edge of the beam on the way down, everything a tumble, a rush to stillness. And for all the speed with which I fell, I landed sooner than I had expected, as though the ground had risen up a bit to meet me. *Thud.* I was an X against the cool, moist dirt.

I wiggled my fingers, my feet, bent my knees, my arms. I opened my eyes. Tree branches stretched out over my head, blurry with the fuzz of new buds. Behind them, the sky was pulled taut, a sheet of blue.

Abby called to me from above, leaning over the edge of the concrete beam, her hands pressed between her knees.

"Are you okay?" she yelled. "Are you okay?" The sun behind her lit the edges of her hair on fire. Her face was an oval shadow. The ground was soft and cool beneath me. I grabbed onto a piece of flat stone embedded in the dirt; it was warm from the sun; it sparkled. I looked up again at the sky, such a deep blue, and I knew this one thing: I was fine.

"I'm fine," I told my friend long-distance. "Really, I'm fine." And though my boyfriend — the one you have read about, the one I had hoped to marry — had just left me for another woman, and though my father was dying of a terrible illness, a disease that bit by bit rendered his body useless — infuriating, idiot flesh that would not hear the brain's commands — I was not lying or covering up when I told her this.

And I am not lying to you, either. I want you to know that.

Because really, when you think about it, I *am* fine. I am that eight-year-old girl, lying on her back, having fallen, rolling over, kneeling, getting ready, once more, to stand. There are days now and then when I think I will not rise, when my knees feel too weak, when I feel too buffeted and beaten, too weary, too damned sad. But underneath all that is the knowledge that I will do it: my body is something marvelous, it is strong, it is dense, I will get up and carry myself forward.

And isn't this what we are all doing, isn't this our work, isn't this what it means to be human, alive: to be jumping and then falling, jumping and falling, gently shaking out our limbs, searching for abrasions, prodding for broken bones, picking ourselves up again? Old wounds open and close and then open once more. We orient ourselves on this planet, we get lost. After a thousand missteps, we find ourselves, we find our way back to the homes we have made for ourselves, homes we build and build again, each time knowing more, knowing less, about the architecture of the planet, its physics, about the way that structures collapse or stand firm, about the way that beams support each other, or fracture beneath an unfair weight, about the way that gravity pulls us, draws us down, trips us up, but keeps us rooted, too, our feet planted on good solid ground.

And this is where I am, where we are, you and I: anchoring ourselves in a spinning world, falling away from ourselves and then back again, all of the past propelling us forward, propelling us onward, searching, squinting into the warmth of a searing sun.

Epilogue

I got another dog a few years ago and named her Harriet. My mother, of course, was insulted when she found out. She prefers to call her Gertrude instead.

What she doesn't see is how much I love that creature, how it soothes me to pick her up, hold her in my arms, stroke her wavy hair, how satisfying it is to provide her with a sense of security, a safe place.

She was a shelter dog; she had come from an abusive home. She didn't trust me at first. Now when I smile at her, her plume of a tail wags so hard it kicks up a wind.

Sometimes I want to hold my mother that close. I want to run my fingers through her wavy hair, once dark, now gray, the cut the same as it was when I was six, the cowlicks as pronounced as ever, but her neck — in my fantasy — finally relaxed, her head heavy against my chest.

· · · · · · · · · · · ·

My father died recently. We think of death as the ultimate separation: my father is gone from me, gone from me, gone. Still, I sometimes feel his presence, he surrounds me, and it is both blessing and curse: I feel strengthened, I feel an energy running through me. But also this: crowded out, watched.

· · · · · · · · · · · ·

After Alex left me, it was a long and awful summer. I felt as though I had been shattered. But I wasn't shattered, really. It was quite a discovery.

There was grieving, repair. The grieving was in part a way of hanging on; it was connection. Recovery — that meant he was really gone.

Then an amazing thing happened: he came back to me. But more important: we found a way back to each other, through the pain and sadness and anger. We stitched our wounds; we delicately closed the holes and put nice seams on the ragged tears. It was a process that made us stronger together; it bound us to each other.

Sometimes he held the needle, and I let him sew me up.

. . . .

It is summer again now, and as I type I can see the scars on my forearm — shiny white nicks against browned skin. I like to look at them. They are a mark of regeneration; they show me how skin can sew itself up, how a split can be repaired. They connect me to myself, to the memory of who I was. They remind me of my history, everything bringing me to this point in time, healing me, making me whole.

. . . .

I remember studying vocabulary in seventh grade and finding out that the word *cleave* meant split as well as cling. It seemed so strange to me at the time that one word could stand for opposite things.

Now it makes sense to me, how the two processes could get so muddled you might as well call them the same thing, how in reality when we pull away we come back too.

It is never a clean break, we are not equipped with the appropriate tools, the necessary single-mindedness, like the butcher with his gleaming blade at the kosher shop my mother used to take me to when I was small, our fingers intertwined as we stood waiting at the counter, and the steel cut so decisively through bone.

Sightline Books
The Iowa Series in Literary Nonfiction